POLICIES AND PAIN:

A PERSONAL AND PHILOSOPHICAL QUEST FOR REFORM

Dr. Spencer M Dayton

DAYTON

For more information, or to book an event, contact:
Spencer@spencermdayton.com

Printed in the United States of America.

Cover design by Spencer M Dayton

Published By
Seraphic Quill House

Hardback ISBN: 979-8-9909404-0-6
Paperback ISBN: 979-8-9909404-2-0
Digital ISBN: 979-8-9909404-1-3

US Copyright Registration Number:
TXu002430916

First Edition: June 2024

Table of Contents

DAYTON

Introduction

THE MORAL IMPERATIVE

In an era marked by profound societal inequities, the pursuit of justice and human rights remains a moral imperative. The very foundations of our societies are being questioned, and new philosophies are needed to guide us through these turbulent times. This treatise emerges from a need to reimagine our moral landscape, offering a philosophical framework that draws on the rich traditions of leftist thought to address some of the most pressing issues of our age.

At the heart of this work lies a simple yet profound question: How can we build a society rooted in justice, equity, and human dignity? In seeking answers, this book examines a broad range of societal challenges, from universal healthcare and wealth redistribution to environmental justice and civil rights, presenting both a philosophical reflection and a practical call to action.

Philosophy has always been intertwined with the public sphere, offering insights that transcend the academic realm and shape the course of nations. This treatise builds on that legacy, advocating for an approach that integrates moral philosophy with concrete policy solutions. By engaging deeply with the thoughts of influential philosophers, both historical and contemporary, we aim to illuminate the ethical dimensions of governance and community life.

Purpose and Scope

This book serves as a treatise on moral and leftist philosophy, divided into thematic chapters that explore critical societal questions. Each chapter tackles a specific issue, ranging from healthcare to labor rights, offering philosophical arguments, historical context, and actionable solutions. By weaving together theoretical reflections and practical advocacy, this work aspires to bridge the gap between philosophy and policy, urging readers to engage not only intellectually but also practically with the ideas presented.

A Call to Action

Philosophy is not merely a theoretical endeavor but a guiding light for societal transformation. This treatise seeks to inspire both intellectual engagement and practical action, offering readers a framework for understanding and addressing the moral imperatives of our time. In doing so, it builds on the rich traditions of moral philosophy, advocating for a world where justice, equity, and human dignity are not just ideals but lived realities.

CHAPTER 1

THE PHILOSOPHY OF HEALTHCARE

Historical Perspectives on Healthcare

The philosophy of healthcare, deeply intertwined with the moral and ethical principles that govern societies, offers a revealing lens into how civilizations have understood and managed the health and well-being of their citizens. This narrative is not just a series of medical advancements; it's a profound exploration of evolving societal values and the corresponding responsibilities toward individual health.

The journey begins in ancient civilizations where healthcare was inextricably linked to spiritual and religious beliefs. In ancient Egypt, health care was predominantly the domain of priests who practiced medicine based on spiritual mandates. Health issues were often interpreted as divine retribution or favor, placing a significant emphasis on moral and spiritual purity as determinants of health. This early integration of health with spirituality highlights how the Egyptians viewed healthcare not just as a physical necessity but as a deeply moral practice.

This spiritual view of health was significantly altered by the Greeks, particularly with the contributions of Hippocrates, who is often regarded as the 'Father of Medicine.' Hippocrates pioneered the idea that diseases had natural causes and should be treated through empirical observation and natural remedies. This was a radical departure from the mystical explanations of the past and laid the groundwork for a rational approach to medicine. It emphasized the human body's natural processes and introduced the concept that healthcare should be based on knowledge and science rather than spiritual or religious interpretation.

The philosophical landscape of healthcare further evolved with the contributions of Plato and Aristotle. Plato's assertion in The Republic that the health of the guardian class was critical for the state's stability introduced an early form of state responsibility in healthcare. However, Plato's perspective was utilitarian, focusing on the health of rulers and soldiers as instrumental to the state's interests. Aristotle, through his concept of eudaimonia or flourishing in Nicomachean Ethics, expanded this view to consider the well-being of the individual as central to their capacity to function and contribute to society. Aristotle's thoughts introduced the idea that a healthy citizenry is crucial for the functioning of a virtuous state, thereby broadening the scope of who should benefit from healthcare.

The Middle Ages brought about a shift where healthcare was heavily influenced by Christian theological values. Healthcare during this era was largely administered by religious institutions, emphasizing care for the sick as a form of Christian charity rather than a civic right. However, these institutions laid the groundwork for the secularization of healthcare, transitioning from purely religious charity to a more community-oriented approach. This evolution marked a significant shift towards viewing healthcare as a societal obligation—a philosophy that was further refined during the Renaissance.

During the Renaissance, an increased emphasis on humanism and scientific inquiry led to significant advancements in medical knowledge. Thinkers like Francis Bacon advocated for the empirical method in science, which significantly influenced medical practice. This period began to recognize health as a collective responsibility of society, setting the stage for Enlightenment philosophers to argue more explicitly for healthcare as a fundamental human right.

Enlightenment thinkers like John Locke and Jean-Jacques Rousseau articulated strong arguments regarding the role of the state in preserving the health of its citizens. Locke's theories suggested that protecting life and, by extension, health was a primary function of government. Rousseau, discussing health within the framework of social contract theory, argued that a just society must ensure the health and well-being of its citizens as part of their social contract.

This philosophical foundation paved the way for the modern conception of healthcare as a right. The 19th and early 20th centuries, marked by industrialization and the rise of the labor movement, saw public health emerge as a major concern. The industrial revolution brought about severe health crises for the working class, which in turn fostered a stronger advocacy for the state's role in managing public health.

This period highlighted the need for systemic healthcare reforms, which were increasingly viewed not just as beneficial but as essential for ensuring the general welfare of the populace.

Today's debates around universal healthcare draw heavily on these historical and philosophical developments. Modern discussions often reference the principles set forth by Enlightenment philosophers, viewing healthcare through the lens of social contracts and human rights. Additionally, contemporary philosophers like John Rawls have influenced these debates by arguing that a just society is one that arranges social and economic inequalities such that they benefit the least advantaged. This principle strongly supports the argument for universal healthcare as not only a moral imperative but also a necessary condition for justice and equity.

By tracing the philosophical evolution of healthcare from ancient spiritual practices to contemporary rights-based arguments, it becomes evident that the concept of healthcare has been a central theme in the dialogue about justice, equity, and the role of the state. Understanding this evolution helps frame current healthcare debates within a broader historical and philosophical context, providing insights into how we might continue to develop healthcare policies that reflect our highest moral and ethical standards.

The Moral Imperatives of Universal Healthcare

The debate surrounding universal healthcare is deeply rooted in the moral imperatives of equity, justice, and the common good, principles that not only define ethical governance but also embody a society's commitment to its citizens. The conception of healthcare as a fundamental human right emerges from a philosophical inquiry that prioritizes human dignity and seeks to address the inequalities inherent in healthcare access and quality.

At the heart of the ethical argument for universal healthcare is the principle of equity. This principle dictates that every individual, regardless of economic status, race, or gender, deserves access to healthcare services. This is not merely a reflection of a society's benevolence but a fundamental acknowledgment of the inherent value of each person. John Rawls' theory of justice, which advocates for structures that benefit the least advantaged in society, supports this view robustly. According to Rawls, a just society is one that adjusts its inequalities in such a way that they maximize the welfare of its most vulnerable members. Healthcare, being essential to survival and quality of life, fits squarely within this ethical framework.

Amartya Sen's capability approach expands this notion by insisting that justice involves more than formal equality; it requires creating conditions where individuals can pursue a life they have reason to value. Health is a prerequisite for many aspects of life that individuals value—whether it is work, education, or social interaction. Without adequate health, the capability of individuals to participate fully in society diminishes, which in turn perpetuates cycles of poverty and disadvantage. Martha Nussbaum further develops this approach by listing bodily health among the central capabilities that a just society must support. From this perspective, universal healthcare is not just a moral obligation but a necessary condition for any society that claims to advance human development and equity.

Moreover, the concept of the common good provides a strong foundation for universal healthcare. This concept argues that certain goods, such as public safety, clean air, and indeed health, are so fundamentally important to society's functioning that they must be universally accessible. Thomas Aquinas argued that justice is not served unless the common good is promoted. In modern times, this argument is bolstered by public health data showing that diseases know no social boundaries; the health of the individual affects the community, and vice versa. Vaccinations, for example, rely on widespread coverage to prevent outbreaks, illustrating how individual health is interconnected with public health.

Additionally, the economic implications of health as a common good are significant. A healthy population fosters economic stability by reducing healthcare costs, increasing productivity, and promoting long-term economic growth. Studies consistently show that preventative care, which is more accessible under universal healthcare systems, reduces the need for expensive emergency care and helps maintain a healthier workforce. Thus, the investment in universal healthcare is not only a moral imperative but also an economically wise policy.

Global health equity is another critical dimension of this discussion. In an increasingly interconnected world, the health of one nation can affect the health of others. This global perspective necessitates policies that extend beyond national borders, promoting healthcare initiatives that address disparities and improve health outcomes worldwide. The principles of distributive justice demand that wealthier countries support health improvements in less developed nations, not only out of altruism but also as a practical measure to ensure global health security. Philosophers like Peter Singer and Thomas Pogge have argued that the affluent have moral obligations to address preventable suffering worldwide, including preventable health issues.

The moral imperatives for universal healthcare are robust and multifaceted. Grounded in the principles of equity, justice, the common good, and global ethical responsibility, these arguments compellingly advocate for healthcare systems that ensure universal access to medical services. By doing so, societies not only uphold their moral duties but also promote broader social and economic well-being. The push for universal healthcare, therefore, is deeply philosophical, rooted in a vision of society that values each individual's health as a cornerstone of justice and human flourishing. Advocating for universal healthcare is advocating for a society that places immense value on life, dignity, and the pursuit of well-being for all.

Universal Healthcare: A Practical Necessity

The push for universal healthcare is often framed within moral parameters, but equally compelling are the practical necessities it addresses. Across the globe, evidence mounts that universal healthcare systems not only improve health outcomes but also contribute to economic stability and social equality.

One of the most compelling arguments for universal healthcare is its proven impact on overall public health. Countries with universal healthcare systems, such as Canada, Sweden, and the United Kingdom, consistently report higher life expectancies and lower infant mortality rates compared to countries without such systems. These outcomes are not coincidental but are direct results of providing comprehensive medical access to all citizens regardless of their economic status. For instance, preventive care—easily accessible in a universal system—greatly reduces the incidence of preventable diseases, which in turn minimizes the need for more complex and costly medical interventions later.

Moreover, universal healthcare systems are designed to be cost-effective. By pooling risk across the entire population, these systems can negotiate better rates for services and medications, achieving economies of scale that individual insurance plans cannot. This collective bargaining power is crucial in keeping medical costs under control, which is evident in the lower per capita healthcare spending seen in countries with universal coverage compared to those without. For example, despite its high standard of healthcare, the United States, which lacks a universal healthcare system, spends significantly more per capita on healthcare than countries with universal systems.

The economic benefits extend beyond cost savings. Universal healthcare contributes to greater economic productivity and stability by ensuring that all citizens are healthy enough to participate in the workforce. Sick workers who delay treatment due to cost concerns often end up taking longer absences from work, reducing overall productivity. Furthermore, medical bankruptcy, a significant issue in countries without universal healthcare, is virtually nonexistent in countries with such systems. By removing the financial barriers to healthcare, families can invest in education, housing, and other needs that contribute to economic growth, instead of depleting their savings on medical bills.

Another practical benefit of universal healthcare is its role in addressing health equity. Disparities in health outcomes are not just a challenge for individuals but a systemic issue that affects entire communities, particularly marginalized groups. Universal healthcare systems are better equipped to address these disparities by ensuring that all citizens, regardless of background or income level, have access to the same quality of care. This is especially critical in diverse societies where socioeconomic disparities often correlate with racial and ethnic disparities in health outcomes.

Furthermore, the global interconnectedness of today's world underscores the practical need for universal healthcare. International travel and trade mean that public health issues in one country can quickly become global concerns. Universal healthcare systems are more effective in managing public health emergencies, such as pandemics, because they can ensure swift and comprehensive responses across the entire population. This was evident during the COVID-19 pandemic, where countries with robust universal healthcare systems generally managed to provide better outcomes through more coordinated and inclusive health service delivery.

The case for universal healthcare extends well beyond ethical imperatives; it is also a matter of practical necessity. The benefits—ranging from improved public health, economic savings, and productivity to greater health equity and effective management of public health emergencies—present a compelling argument for the adoption of universal healthcare systems globally. These systems not only fulfill a moral duty to ensure health for all but also serve as foundational elements for stable, productive, and equitable societies.

Philosophical Foundations for Healthcare Policy

The application of philosophical principles to healthcare policy is not merely academic; it translates into actionable and beneficial healthcare practices that resonate with a society's moral and ethical standards. The philosophical foundations that advocate for universal healthcare—equity, justice, and the common good—are vital in shaping policies that not only address health as a basic human right but also ensure the sustainability and effectiveness of healthcare systems.

Ethical theories provide a substantial basis for healthcare policy, urging policymakers to consider not only the outcomes but the fairness of their strategies. For instance, the principle of distributive justice, which concerns the equitable allocation of resources, is central to the development of policies that ensure all individuals have access to necessary medical services without discrimination. This principle is particularly important in the allocation of limited resources, such as during vaccine rollouts or in the distribution of life-saving treatments, where decisions must reflect not only medical needs but also a commitment to fairness and equality.

Moreover, the utilitarian approach, which seeks the greatest good for the greatest number, can also guide healthcare policies, especially in preventive care and public health initiatives. For example, vaccination programs and public health campaigns aimed at preventing diseases like diabetes or heart disease are designed to maximize overall health benefits for the population. These programs, often resulting from utilitarian calculations, highlight how a focus on community-wide benefits can drive policy decisions that profoundly impact public health.

The capability approach further enriches healthcare policy by emphasizing the enhancement of individual capabilities as a goal of healthcare provision. Policies informed by this perspective focus on providing individuals with the necessary health services that allow them to achieve personal well-being and contribute effectively to society. For instance, mental health services and rehabilitative programs are designed not just to treat diseases but to restore or enhance individuals' abilities to function and participate in their communities, reflecting a deep commitment to improving individual life conditions as a matter of policy.

In addition to these theoretical underpinnings, practical implementations of these philosophical principles can be observed in various healthcare reforms around the world. The Health Care Reform Act in Germany, for example, which aims at balancing cost, accessibility, and quality of healthcare, mirrors the principles of equity and justice by ensuring that every citizen has comprehensive health coverage while maintaining the system's sustainability through efficient resource management.

Similarly, in Taiwan, the introduction of a universal health insurance system in 1995 was grounded in principles of universal access and equity. This system has successfully provided high-quality medical care to the entire population at a relatively low cost, demonstrating the practical viability of philosophically driven healthcare policies.

The influence of philosophical thought on healthcare policy underscores the importance of ethical considerations in policy formulation. By grounding healthcare policies in philosophical doctrines that promote justice, equity, and the common good, societies can create healthcare systems that are not only effective and sustainable but also reflective of their moral commitments. These systems then serve as critical frameworks within which individuals can pursue healthier, more productive lives, ultimately contributing to a more just and equitable society.

Counterarguments and Philosophical Rebuttals

While universal healthcare garners strong philosophical and empirical support, it is not without its detractors who raise concerns about efficiency, cost, freedom of choice, and quality of care. Each of these concerns warrants careful consideration and a response grounded in the same philosophical rigor that advocates for universal healthcare.

Critics often claim that universal healthcare systems are inherently inefficient, plagued by bureaucratic red tape that can lead to sluggish services and long waiting times. This critique is typically contrasted with the perceived efficiency of market-driven systems. However, empirical evidence from countries with universal healthcare systems often tells a different story, showing that these systems can deliver superior health outcomes at lower per capita costs than systems relying on private insurance. From a utilitarian perspective, which prioritizes the greatest good for the greatest number, the trade-off of slower services for some procedures is reasonable if the outcome is comprehensive coverage for all. Furthermore, the administrative overhead in private insurance systems, which includes expenses related to marketing and profit, often exceeds that in more centralized public systems. Thus, while no system is without delays, the efficiency argument against universal healthcare may not fully account for the inefficiencies and high costs associated with privatized care.

Another frequently voiced concern is the cost associated with implementing and maintaining a universal healthcare system. Critics argue that such systems impose an unsustainable tax burden on citizens. This argument can be countered by appealing to the principle of distributive justice, which advocates for a fair distribution of society's burdens and benefits. An investment in universal healthcare is not merely an expenditure but a critical investment in public health, which in turn promotes a healthier, more productive workforce. This broader societal benefit justifies the costs, reflecting a nation's commitment to the well-being of all its citizens, particularly the most vulnerable. The ethical framework of universal healthcare, therefore, supports such investment as a manifestation of societal values of equity and compassion.

The issue of freedom of choice is also a significant point of contention. Opponents of universal healthcare often argue that such systems limit individuals' ability to choose their healthcare providers, thus infringing on personal freedom. However, this argument can be reevaluated by considering the concept of positive liberty, which is the freedom to live a life one values, facilitated by access to essential services like healthcare.

Universal healthcare expands individual freedom by alleviating the burden of healthcare costs, thus enabling people to pursue their life goals more fully. In this sense, while some choice might be restricted, the essential choice of accessing health services when needed is significantly enhanced, broadening actual freedoms rather than constricting them.

Lastly, the concern that universal healthcare could compromise the quality of care is often cited by its critics. They suggest that a system accessible to all might lead to a dilution of quality due to resource constraints. However, universal healthcare systems around the world have stringent regulations and standards designed to ensure high-quality medical care. These systems aim to provide a baseline of quality care for every citizen, which in many instances has led to an overall improvement in public health outcomes. Ethically, guaranteeing that everyone receives adequate healthcare—even if it means the very wealthy might not have access to certain luxuries—is a reflection of a commitment to equality and justice. Ensuring that all citizens receive quality healthcare demonstrates a society's dedication to fairness and the well-being of its populace.

In addressing these criticisms, it becomes clear that the philosophical underpinnings supporting universal healthcare not only advocate for its implementation based on moral grounds but also robustly defend against common counterarguments. By carefully examining and responding to these critiques, advocates of universal healthcare can strengthen their case, demonstrating that such systems are not only ethically sound but also pragmatically viable.

CHAPTER 2

WEALTH AND MORAL ECONOMY

The exploration of wealth and its impact on society is a central theme that has intrigued philosophers and economists throughout history. From ancient times to the modern era, the question of how wealth should be distributed within societies has sparked intense debate and differing viewpoints. This section delves into these philosophical discussions, tracing the evolution of economic thought and its implications for understanding wealth in contemporary society.

In ancient Greece, the philosophical foundations of economic thought were laid by thinkers like Plato and Aristotle, who pondered the role of wealth in achieving a well-ordered society. Plato, in his "Republic," envisioned a society where the guardians, the ruling class, were not motivated by personal wealth but by the pursuit of justice and common good. He proposed that the guardians should live communally with shared resources to prevent wealth from corrupting their judgment. Aristotle, on the other hand, recognized the necessity of private property but emphasized moderation and the virtue of generosity. He argued that wealth should be used to promote virtuous living and community welfare, a concept that laid early groundwork for thinking about economic justice.

These classical ideas were further developed during the Middle Ages, where Christian thinkers like Thomas Aquinas integrated Aristotelian philosophy with Christian doctrine. Aquinas argued that while private property was natural, its use must ultimately serve the common good. He posited that true charity involved distributing one's excess wealth to those in need, thus introducing a moral imperative to economic actions.

The Renaissance and Enlightenment periods brought significant shifts in economic philosophy with the rise of mercantilism and early capitalism. Thinkers like Adam Smith revolutionized economic thought by advocating for the 'invisible hand' of the free market, suggesting that individual self-interest, rather than centralized planning, often resulted in the most efficient allocation of resources. However, Smith also warned of the dangers of unchecked wealth accumulation and the potential for moral decay if economic activities were disengaged from ethical considerations. In the 19th century, Karl Marx presented a radical critique of capitalism, arguing that the system inherently led to the exploitation of the working class and the concentration of wealth in the hands of a few. Marx's theory of economic determinism and class struggle provided a new lens through which to view wealth distribution, emphasizing the role of economic structures in shaping societal relations and the potential for revolutionary change to establish a more equitable distribution of resources.

The 20th century introduced further complexities with the emergence of global capitalism and advanced industrial economies. John Maynard Keynes and later economists advocated for government intervention in the market to prevent economic inequalities and stabilize economies. Keynesian economics, with its emphasis on regulating economic cycles and redistributing wealth through taxation and government spending, reflected a practical application of philosophical principles to manage wealth distribution more equitably.

Today, the debate continues as modern philosophers and economists grapple with the challenges of wealth inequality, globalization, and the sustainability of capitalist models. Contemporary thinkers like John Rawls have reintroduced notions of social justice into economic discussions, arguing for a theoretical framework where societal arrangements, including the distribution of wealth, are organized to benefit the least advantaged. Rawls' ideas have spurred a renewed interest in the ethical dimensions of economic policies and the moral responsibilities of governments and individuals.

The discussion of wealth and its role in society is thus deeply rooted in philosophical inquiry. From the ideal states envisioned by Plato to modern theories of economic justice, the evolution of economic thought reflects a continual quest to balance material prosperity with ethical considerations. This historical journey not only informs our understanding of wealth distribution but also challenges us to consider how contemporary economic systems can better reflect our deepest values about fairness, justice, and the common good.

This exploration sets the stage for a deeper discussion on the ethics of wealth redistribution and progressive taxation, linking historical philosophical insights with modern economic challenges.

The Ethics of Wealth Distribution

Building upon the historical and philosophical context outlined in the discussion of wealth's impact on society, we now turn our focus to the ethics of wealth redistribution. This examination delves into both classical and contemporary philosophical debates, arguing for the moral imperative of reducing economic inequalities through deliberate measures like redistribution.

The principle of redistributing wealth is grounded in a variety of ethical frameworks that advocate for a more equitable allocation of resources within society. Central to these discussions is the notion that true social justice cannot be achieved without addressing the disparities that prevent significant portions of the population from achieving their full potential. Philosophers have long wrestled with the question of whether and how to redistribute wealth, proposing various theories that justify such practices on moral, ethical, and practical grounds.

John Rawls, one of the most influential modern philosophers in this area, proposed the concept of "justice as fairness." Rawls argued that social and economic inequalities should be arranged so that they are to the greatest benefit of the least advantaged members of society. This principle, known as the difference principle, supports wealth redistribution as a means to ensure that everyone has the minimum resources necessary to participate in society and pursue their own goals. According to Rawls, a just society uses redistributive measures to level the playing field, ensuring that everyone has access to basic liberties and opportunities regardless of their initial position in society.

Rawls' ideas have sparked extensive debate and have been instrumental in shaping contemporary views on social justice and public policy. They challenge us to consider not just the outcomes of economic inequality but also the processes that lead to these outcomes. By focusing on the structures of society that perpetuate inequality—such as laws, policies, and practices that favor the wealthy—Rawls' framework pushes for systemic changes that address the root causes of economic disparity.

Complementing Rawlsian theory are the ethical arguments that stem from utilitarianism, which advocates for actions that maximize the overall happiness or well-being of the population. From a utilitarian perspective, wealth redistribution can be justified if it results in a greater overall level of societal well-being, even if it means diminishing the wealth of the richest. This view suggests that redistributing wealth from the richest to the poorer segments of society can lead to a more harmonious and stable society, as it reduces the extremes of wealth and poverty that can lead to social unrest and dissatisfaction.

However, philosophical support for wealth redistribution is not without its critics. Some argue from a libertarian standpoint that redistributive policies infringe on individual freedoms, particularly the rights to private property and to the fruits of one's labor. These critics maintain that the state should play a minimal role in the economic lives of its citizens, advocating for voluntary charity as an alternative to mandated redistribution.

Addressing these criticisms, proponents of redistribution argue that economic rights cannot be fully separated from other social and political rights. They suggest that in the absence of a basic level of material well-being, other rights—such as the right to vote, the right to education, and even the right to life—can be rendered meaningless. Thus, the redistribution of wealth is not merely a matter of economic policy but a fundamental prerequisite for the effective participation in democratic society and the full exercise of civil rights.

The ethical arguments for and against wealth redistribution also extend to the practical implications of such policies. Empirical evidence from various countries shows that societies with less economic inequality tend to have better overall health outcomes, higher levels of education, and greater social cohesion. These benefits suggest that redistribution, when done effectively, can contribute not only to individual well-being but also to the broader societal good.

In synthesizing these philosophical perspectives, it becomes clear that the debate over wealth redistribution is as much about values and ethical principles as it is about economic theories and outcomes. As we continue to confront growing global inequality, the philosophical discussions surrounding wealth distribution remain critically important in guiding our approaches to crafting fairer, more just societies. This dialogue challenges us to think deeply about the kind of world we want to live in and the roles that justice, equity, and compassion should play in shaping our collective future.

Progressive Taxation and Economic Reforms

The discourse on wealth redistribution naturally leads to a focused discussion on progressive taxation as a practical tool for achieving social equity. Progressive taxation, where the tax rate increases as the taxable amount rises, has been advocated by many as a means to balance the economic scales and fund public services that benefit all citizens.

This section explores the philosophical justifications for progressive taxation and considers its broader implications for economic reforms aimed at addressing inequality.

Progressive taxation is rooted in the principle that those who have more should contribute more to the societal infrastructure that supports their success. This concept is not merely about fairness but also about the practical responsibility of supporting a society that fosters opportunity for all its members. The rationale behind progressive taxation aligns with the ethical theories that prioritize distributive justice, as articulated by philosophers like John Rawls. According to Rawls, a society arranged to benefit the least advantaged, and that mitigates inequalities that do not benefit all, is a more just society. Progressive taxation serves this purpose by redistributing wealth more equitably and funding essential services like education, healthcare, and social security, which help level the playing field.

From a utilitarian perspective, progressive taxation can be seen as a way to maximize societal happiness. By taxing the wealthy at higher rates, the government can prevent the diminishing marginal utility of wealth. The wealthy experience a lesser decrease in happiness from the loss of a dollar than the poor, who gain significant benefits from each additional dollar. Thus, redistributing this wealth through social programs can lead to a greater overall level of well-being across society.

However, the implementation of progressive taxation often sparks vigorous debate about its impact on economic growth and individual freedoms. Critics argue that high tax rates on the wealthy could stifle innovation and entrepreneurship by reducing the incentives to earn more. They contend that this could lead to an overall economic slowdown, which ultimately harms society. Furthermore, there is the argument of property rights that suggests individuals should have the right to retain the wealth they legally acquire without excessive government interference.

Addressing these concerns, proponents of progressive taxation argue that the benefits of a more equitable society, with reduced levels of poverty and increased opportunities for all, can lead to a more stable and productive economy. Moreover, historical data from periods of high economic growth in various countries often correlate with higher tax rates on the wealthiest, suggesting that economic prosperity does not necessarily decline with higher taxation. This evidence challenges the notion that progressive taxation harms economic vitality.

Additionally, progressive taxation is not just about redistributing income but about contributing to a collective investment in public goods that benefit society as a whole. Quality education, robust healthcare systems, and reliable infrastructure support economic activity and contribute to a stable environment where businesses can thrive, and individuals can lead healthier, more productive lives.

The debate over progressive taxation also brings into focus broader economic reforms that aim to mitigate inequality. Policies such as minimum wage laws, universal basic income, and subsidized education are often funded by revenues from progressive taxes. These measures are grounded in the philosophy that economic security and access to basic services should not be privileges reserved for the wealthy but basic rights accessible to all. Such reforms are seen not only as corrections to market failures but also as necessary steps towards a more equitable society where everyone has the opportunity to succeed.

In conclusion, progressive taxation and the associated economic reforms represent practical applications of philosophical principles aimed at achieving greater social equity. They embody a society's commitment to reducing disparities and improving the quality of life for all its members, fostering a more cohesive and just community. This discussion underscores the importance of considering both the ethical underpinnings and practical outcomes of tax policies as we strive to build fairer economic systems.

Philosophical Critiques and Contemporary Alternatives

In addressing the challenges and inequalities perpetuated by traditional capitalist systems, there is a growing discourse around alternative economic models that promise a fairer and more equitable distribution of wealth. These alternatives challenge the fundamental tenets of capitalism, particularly the notions of private property and profit maximization, advocating for systems that prioritize social welfare and community benefits over individual gain.

One prominent alternative is the model of democratic socialism, which advocates for major industries and resources to be owned and controlled by the state or by the workers themselves. This model aims to prevent the accumulation of wealth in the hands of a few and ensures that the economic benefits of production are distributed more evenly across society. Democratic socialism also emphasizes the importance of democratic processes not just in political governance but also in economic decision-making, allowing workers and communities to have a say in how their workplaces and economic institutions are run. This approach is underpinned by the belief that economic decisions should be made in a manner that benefits the majority and supports the common good, rather than serving the interests of a small elite.

Cooperativism is another economic model that offers a radical departure from traditional capitalist structures. In cooperative businesses, ownership and decision-making powers are shared among all members, and profits are distributed more equitably according to each member's contribution or democratically decided policies. This model fosters a sense of solidarity and mutual aid, as members work together not just to profit but to create sustainable and community-oriented businesses. Cooperatives are often seen as more resilient to economic downturns because they prioritize long-term community welfare over short-term profits.

The concept of a mixed economy is also gaining traction as a viable alternative. In a mixed economic system, some sectors are left to private ownership and free market mechanisms, while others, particularly those that are critical to national security or public welfare (like healthcare, transportation, and utilities), are controlled by the government. This model seeks to combine the efficiency and innovation spurred by the free market with the stability and equity provided by government intervention. It acknowledges the role of the market in driving economic growth but also recognizes the government's responsibility to correct market failures and ensure that the basic needs of its citizens are met.

Each of these models addresses the inherent shortcomings of pure capitalism, particularly its tendency to produce significant economic and social inequalities. By redistributing control and profits more equitably, these alternatives aim to create economic systems that are not only more just but also more sustainable. They challenge us to rethink the relationship between economic activity and social progress, advocating for systems that better reflect the values of equity, participation, and sustainability.

The exploration of these alternative economic models is crucial in the broader quest for economic justice. As the global economy continues to evolve, the dialogue about these alternatives provides valuable insights into how different economic structures can impact societal well-being. It prompts a reevaluation of current economic policies and encourages a more holistic approach to understanding the interplay between economic systems and social outcomes.

This discourse not only enriches our understanding of possible economic configurations but also aligns with a philosophical commitment to exploring diverse avenues for achieving a more equitable world. By considering these alternatives, we can better assess the potential for creating economic systems that truly serve the broader interests of society, ensuring that wealth and resources are used to enhance the lives of all, not just a privileged few.

CHAPTER 3

ENVIRONMENTAL ETHICS AND JUSTICE

Environmental justice is not merely a policy initiative but a profound moral and philosophical challenge that addresses the intersections of environmental health, social equity, and human rights. This chapter introduces the concept of environmental justice, exploring its philosophical significance and its roots in broader movements for social justice. The urgency of environmental justice becomes evident when we consider how environmental issues—from climate change to pollution—disproportionately impact the most vulnerable populations globally.

The idea of environmental justice emerged prominently in the late 20th century, catalyzed by activism from communities who found themselves on the front lines of environmental degradation. These communities, often economically disadvantaged and racially marginalized, faced the brunt of harmful environmental practices, from toxic waste dumps to disproportionate rates of asthma due to polluted air. The grassroots efforts to combat these injustices laid the groundwork for recognizing environmental justice as a critical element of global human rights discussions.

Central to the discussion of environmental justice is the philosophical exploration of how our environmental practices intersect with principles of fairness, equity, and the common good. This integration of environmental concerns with social justice challenges traditional environmentalism—which often focused solely on conservation and preservation—to consider who is most affected by environmental policies. It compels us to ask: Who benefits from environmental exploitation, and who suffers? How do our environmental decisions reflect our values about human life and dignity?

Philosophically, environmental justice is deeply rooted in theories of distributive justice, which are concerned with the fair allocation of resources and burdens. Thinkers like John Rawls have argued that societies should be structured in such a way that they compensate for inequalities, ensuring that the least advantaged are not unduly burdened. Applying this to environmental policies means creating systems where the costs of environmental damage and the benefits of environmental resources are distributed more equitably. This is particularly relevant in contexts where poor and minority communities bear the environmental costs of industrial progress from which they gain little benefit.

Moreover, environmental justice is informed by the concept of the intrinsic value of nature proposed by philosophers like Aldo Leopold, who in his "land ethic," suggested that the environment itself, apart from human interests, possesses a moral worth that obliges us to treat it with respect. This view challenges purely utilitarian approaches to environmental management and argues for a broader ethical relationship with the natural world.

The interconnections between human rights and environmental health are also key to understanding environmental justice. The right to a healthy environment is increasingly recognized as fundamental to the realization of other human rights, including the rights to health, life, and cultural integrity. For indigenous communities, whose livelihoods and cultural heritage are intimately tied to their environments, environmental degradation can be a direct threat to their survival and identity.

Environmental justice expands the scope of traditional environmental discourse, focusing on the equitable distribution of environmental risks and benefits, the intrinsic value of the natural world, and the integration of environmental health into the framework of human rights. It challenges us to consider not only how we protect the environment but also how we ensure that the benefits of environmental protection are shared by all members of society, particularly those who have historically been marginalized.

Philosophical Foundations of Environmental Ethics

In the context of environmental justice, the philosophical exploration of ethical frameworks provides a robust foundation for understanding the complex relationship between human activity, environmental impact, and social equity. This section delves into the ethical considerations that drive the movement for environmental justice, emphasizing the role of philosophical theories in addressing how climate change exacerbates existing economic and social disparities.

Climate change represents one of the most daunting challenges facing humanity, with its effects manifesting disproportionately among the world's most vulnerable populations. The ethics of environmental justice compel us to consider not only the global nature of climate change but also the localized impacts that exacerbate existing inequalities. Communities that are economically disadvantaged often suffer the greatest from climate change because of their lower capacity to respond to natural disasters, health crises, and economic disruptions that result from environmental degradation.

The philosophical underpinnings of environmental ethics, such as those proposed by thinkers like Aldo Leopold and Peter Singer, emphasize a moral responsibility towards not just other humans but also the broader ecological systems. Leopold's land ethic extends ethical consideration to the land itself, arguing that a truly ethical relationship between humans and the environment includes respecting ecological processes and living sustainably within them. This perspective challenges us to reconsider our environmental impact and recognize the intrinsic value of nature, not merely as a resource to be exploited but as a community to which we belong and for which we are responsible.

Peter Singer's utilitarian approach to environmental ethics, which focuses on the greatest good for the greatest number, further supports the push for environmental justice by highlighting the need for actions that benefit not only current but also future generations. This approach calls for a preventative stance on environmental degradation, arguing that the potential suffering caused by climate change can be averted through equitable and proactive measures.

These ethical considerations are particularly poignant in discussions about global responsibilities and the ethics of care. Wealthier nations, which have historically contributed the most to greenhouse gas emissions, face moral questions about their obligations to less developed countries that are now bearing the brunt of climate change effects. The principles of justice, as discussed by philosophers like John Rawls, suggest that these nations have an obligation to aid those who are least well-off and most affected by environmental injustices.

The discussion of climate debt is also critical here. It encapsulates the idea that richer countries owe a debt to poorer nations for the environmental damage caused by their greater historical emissions. This concept not only acknowledges responsibility but also underscores the need for reparative actions, which can take the form of financial aid, technology transfer, or capacity-building initiatives to help vulnerable countries adapt to and mitigate the impacts of climate change.

Moreover, the principle of the polluter pays, a practical application of environmental ethics, asserts that those who cause environmental damage should be responsible for compensating those affected. This principle is crucial in implementing policies that not only deter excessive pollution but also ensure that the costs of environmental harm are not unjustly imposed on those least able to bear them.

Through these philosophical lenses, the section on climate change and economic disparities in the context of environmental justice illuminates the deep ethical complexities involved in addressing climate change. It challenges us to develop policies and practices that are not only effective in reducing environmental impact but also fundamentally just, ensuring that the burdens and benefits of environmental actions are shared equitably across all sectors of society. This philosophical approach helps to frame the subsequent discussion on sustainable policies and the necessity for global cooperation, guiding us toward solutions that honor our ethical commitments to both current and future generations.

Climate Change and Economic Disparities

Moving forward into a focused discussion of sustainable policies and global cooperation, we examine how governments and international bodies can formulate and implement strategies that promote environmental sustainability while ensuring justice. This section explores the interconnected roles of policy-making and international agreements in fostering an equitable approach to environmental challenges, particularly under the framework of environmental justice.

Sustainable policies are crucial not only for the preservation of environmental resources but also for the promotion of equity and social justice. These policies are designed to meet current needs without compromising the ability of future generations to meet their own, integrating economic, social, and environmental considerations. In the realm of environmental justice, the focus extends beyond sustainability to include the fair distribution of environmental benefits and burdens. This entails creating policies that not only reduce environmental degradation but also ensure that the poorest and most vulnerable populations are protected and uplifted.

Government initiatives can play a pivotal role in this context. National strategies might include stringent pollution controls that protect air and water quality, particularly in areas where disadvantaged communities are disproportionately affected. Renewable energy projects are another key area, reducing dependence on fossil fuels and mitigating climate change while creating job opportunities in new industries. These initiatives often require innovative legislation and strong regulatory frameworks that prioritize public health and welfare over corporate profits.

At the international level, cooperation is essential for addressing environmental issues that cross national borders, such as climate change, biodiversity loss, and oceanic pollution. Global environmental agreements, like the Paris Agreement, serve as frameworks for collective action. They rely on the principles of shared but differentiated responsibilities, recognizing that while climate change is a global problem, not all countries have contributed to it equally, nor do they have the same capabilities to combat it.

Such agreements often include mechanisms for technology transfer and financial support from developed to developing nations, embodying the principle that those who have more resources and have contributed more to environmental degradation have greater responsibilities. These international efforts are crucial in ensuring that smaller or less wealthy nations have the means to implement sustainable practices and adapt to climate change impacts.

However, the success of these policies and agreements heavily depends on their ability to enforce regulations and commitments. Challenges include ensuring compliance from all parties, overcoming political and economic pressures that favor short-term gains over long-term sustainability, and addressing the inherent inequalities that can be exacerbated by poorly implemented environmental policies.

Moreover, the concept of environmental justice demands that these policies and agreements are not only effective but also fair. This includes considering how decisions might disproportionately impact certain communities and ensuring that there is equitable participation in the decision-making process. For instance, indigenous communities often have unique relationships with their environments and may be particularly vulnerable to policies that affect land use and resource rights. Ensuring that these communities have a voice in international forums and in national policy deliberations is key to upholding justice.

In crafting these policies, governments and international bodies must navigate complex ethical landscapes, economic pressures, and varied political wills. However, the moral imperatives discussed in the philosophical foundations of environmental justice provide a clear directive: to create a just and sustainable world, we must develop and enforce policies that not only mitigate harm but also distribute environmental goods in a manner that respects all individuals' rights and dignity.

This exploration into sustainable policies and global cooperation sets the stage for the final discussions in this chapter, which will consider the ongoing challenges and the future direction of environmental justice advocacy. Through this lens, we can better appreciate the intricate balance required to forge policies that are both effective in addressing environmental issues and equitable in their implementation and impact.

Sustainable Policies and Global Cooperation

The journey toward environmental justice is fraught with formidable challenges and marked by ongoing battles against deeply entrenched interests. As this chapter concludes, we reflect on the essential, continuous efforts required to advance this crucial cause. The road ahead demands a steadfast commitment to advocacy, an unwavering dedication to refining policies, and a robust framework for international cooperation. These elements are not merely supportive details but the very pillars upon which the future of environmental justice rests.

Advocacy remains the lifeblood of the environmental justice movement. It is the force that brings marginalized voices to the forefront, challenging the status quo and demanding change. Advocates harness the power of community, using collective action to spotlight injustices and push for solutions that rectify imbalances in environmental burdens and benefits. Their work is vital in ensuring that the plight of the most vulnerable does not fade into the background but resonates in the corridors of power where decisions are made.

Policy refinement is an ongoing necessity in the quest for environmental justice. As the landscape of environmental science and public health evolves, so too must the policies that govern our responses to these issues. This dynamic process requires policymakers to be both responsive and proactive, crafting legislation that not only addresses current needs but anticipates future challenges. The complexity of environmental issues demands policies that are both scientifically sound and socially equitable, ensuring that they serve not only to protect the planet but to uplift those who have historically borne the brunt of environmental neglect.

International cooperation is pivotal in addressing environmental justice on a global scale. Environmental degradation knows no borders, and the impacts of climate change are felt worldwide, often exacerbating vulnerabilities in regions least equipped to manage them. Effective global governance models are required to manage these shared resources and challenges. International agreements and cooperative efforts must be strengthened to ensure they are inclusive, enforceable, and capable of achieving meaningful progress. This involves not only commitments from states but also partnerships that span sectors, involving non-governmental organizations, the private sector, and civil society.

As we consider the path forward, it is clear that the fight for environmental justice is as urgent as it is arduous. This movement calls for a holistic approach that integrates ethical considerations with practical solutions, ensuring that future generations inherit a world that is not only habitable but just. It challenges us to reimagine our relationship with the environment, to conceive of it not as a resource to be exploited but as a shared home to be cherished and preserved for all its inhabitants.

The momentum of environmental justice efforts must not only be maintained but accelerated. As this chapter closes, we are reminded of the resilience and resolve that must define our approach to environmental advocacy. The stakes are high, and the time for decisive action is now. The continued pursuit of environmental justice is not just an environmental or social necessity but a moral imperative that we are compelled to address for the sake of our collective future.

Conclusion

As this chapter on environmental justice concludes, we must recognize that the challenges we face are not just environmental or social issues—they are profound moral imperatives calling for a comprehensive reevaluation of how societies interact with the natural world. This reevaluation demands a paradigm shift in our legal, economic, and cultural frameworks to integrate the principles of justice and sustainability into every facet of environmental governance.

The journey towards environmental justice has laid bare the systemic inequities that permeate our societies. It has shown that the environmental degradation affecting our planet does not do so indiscriminately; rather, it disproportionately impacts those least able to bear its burdens. Addressing this requires more than piecemeal solutions—it necessitates a transformational approach that redefines our relationship with the earth as one of stewardship rather than exploitation.

Moving forward, the path to environmental justice will require robust advocacy, innovative policy-making, and enduring global cooperation. Advocates must continue to amplify the voices of those most affected by environmental injustices, ensuring that these voices are not only heard but heeded in policy circles and boardrooms. Their stories and struggles should inform the creation of policies that are not merely reactive but fundamentally proactive, preventing harm before it occurs.

Policymakers, for their part, must embrace the complexity of these challenges and seek solutions that are as multifaceted as the problems themselves. This involves implementing laws and regulations that do more than enforce minimum standards; they must propel industries towards practices that actively benefit the environment and the communities that depend on it. These policies should encourage a transition to renewable energies, support sustainable agriculture practices, and ensure that economic development does not come at the cost of ecological health.

Internationally, the fight for environmental justice requires concerted efforts across borders. Climate change, pollution, and resource depletion are global phenomena that necessitate a global response. This response must be rooted in principles of fairness and equity, recognizing the different capacities of countries to address environmental issues and the varying impacts these issues have on their populations. International agreements should be not only ambitious in their environmental goals but also equitable in their expectations and supports, ensuring that all nations can contribute to and benefit from global environmental efforts.

Ultimately, the pursuit of environmental justice is a call to envision a future where the environment no longer needs defending because it is woven into the very fabric of our societal structures. It is a vision of a world where the rights to clean air, water, and soil are guaranteed not just in policy documents but in the lived experiences of all people. Achieving this vision will require persistence, creativity, and courage; it will require us to hold ourselves accountable to the ideals of equity and sustainability we espouse.

The discourse on environmental justice outlined in this chapter is more than an academic exercise; it is an urgent call to action. It invites each of us to engage, advocate, and innovate as if our lives and the lives of future generations depend on it—because they do. As we turn the page, let us carry forward the lessons learned, and the commitments forged towards creating a just and sustainable future for all.

CHAPTER 4

WORKERS' RIGHTS

The discourse on workers' rights is an intricate tapestry woven through the fabric of social justice, equity, and human dignity. As we delve into the philosophical dimensions of labor, we unearth a rich historical narrative that stretches from the sweat of the industrial revolution to the contemporary digital age, where new forms of work continually emerge and reshape our understanding of employment. Workers' rights are not merely a facet of economic systems but are central to the realization of equitable and just societies.

The concept of workers' rights has evolved significantly over the centuries, shaped by relentless struggles and the relentless pursuit of equity in the workplace. Early labor movements, catalyzed by the harsh realities of factory life during the industrial revolution, laid the groundwork for the rights workers enjoy today. These movements were not just battles for better wages or shorter hours; they were profound calls for recognition of the workers' humanity, dignity, and worth. Labor activists and thinkers argued that the labor force was not a commodity to be exploited, but a collective of individuals, each deserving respect and fair treatment.

This historical struggle has seen various philosophical underpinnings that have influenced its trajectory. The early dialogues around labor rights were infused with Marxist theories, which highlighted the exploitative dynamics of capitalism and advocated for the proletariat's rights and welfare. Karl Marx's vision of labor as an extension of one's life force and a means of self-actualization brought a deeper, more existential dimension to the discourse on workers' rights, framing the exploitation of workers as not just an economic injustice but a profound moral wrongdoing.

Parallel to the critical views of Marx, the liberal perspectives of philosophers like John Stuart Mill emphasized the importance of liberty and autonomy within the workplace. Mill's advocacy for individual rights echoed the need for protections within the labor market, ensuring that workers were not reduced to mere cogs in an industrial machine but were respected as autonomous individuals capable of contributing thoughtfully and meaningfully to the economic and social fabric.

The evolution of labor movements and the philosophical debates that fueled them have led to significant legal and social reforms. From the establishment of the eight-hour workday to the recognition of collective bargaining rights, the milestones achieved through these movements are testament to the power of organized action and philosophical rigor in confronting injustice.

Today, as we continue to navigate the complexities of a globalized economy, the lessons learned from past labor struggles remain profoundly relevant. They remind us that workers' rights are an ongoing concern, dynamically evolving as the nature of work itself changes. As we engage with this chapter, we embark on an exploration of how contemporary challenges within the labor sector can be addressed through a philosophical lens that values equity, respects dignity, and promotes justice. In doing so, we not only honor the legacy of those who fought for workers' rights but also contribute to a future where these rights are expanded and fully realized.

Philosophical Foundations of Labor Rights

The discourse on workers' rights is deeply rooted in a sophisticated philosophical tradition that critically examines labor's role in human flourishing and social equity. This tradition, enriched by contributions from Karl Marx, John Stuart Mill, Amartya Sen, and Martha Nussbaum, provides a nuanced framework for understanding labor as an essential component of a just society. These thinkers collectively illuminate the profound ethical implications of labor practices, urging a reevaluation that transcends economic considerations to address core human values.

Karl Marx's critique of capitalism elucidates labor as not merely a means to subsistence but as a vital expression of human creativity and agency. Marx exposes how capitalist modes of production alienate workers from their labor, the products they create, and their communal ties. This alienation, Marx argues, is a profound distortion of human nature, as it prevents individuals from realizing their full potential and degrades their quality of life. The implications of Marx's theory extend beyond identifying systemic injustices; they compel a reimagining of labor relations to restore worker autonomy and reengage the human spirit.

For Marx, the capitalist system commodifies labor, reducing workers to mere cogs in the machinery of production. This reduction alienates them from the products of their labor, the production process itself, and their fellow workers, fostering a profound sense of estrangement. By advocating for the abolition of exploitative labor practices and the establishment of a classless society where workers collectively control the means of production, Marx envisioned a world in which individuals could reclaim their creative potential and achieve genuine self-realization. His philosophy, therefore, emphasizes the transformative power of labor when liberated from the fetters of exploitation.

John Stuart Mill's liberal philosophy complements Marx's critiques by emphasizing the necessity of safeguarding individual freedoms within the labor market. Mill articulates a vision of the workplace where personal liberty and mutual respect govern interactions, positing that the protection of workers' rights is essential not only for individual well-being but for the preservation of a democratic society. His advocacy for workers' autonomy and rights to organize forms a cornerstone of liberal labor ethics, highlighting the interdependence of economic practices and democratic values. Mill believed that social progress is intrinsically linked to the moral and intellectual development of individuals, which is undermined when workers are treated as mere instruments of production.

Further expanding the philosophical discourse, Amartya Sen and Martha Nussbaum's capabilities approach reframes labor rights in terms of human development and empowerment. They argue that access to decent work is fundamental to enabling individuals to pursue a life of their choosing and to contribute meaningfully to society. This perspective shifts the focus from labor as an economic necessity to labor as a critical enabler of personal and communal thriving. The capabilities approach insists on policies that do not merely prevent harm but actively foster an environment where all individuals can realize their potential.

Sen emphasizes that labor policies should aim to expand people's freedoms to achieve valuable beings and doings, or "functionings." He argues that an individual's ability to work in a safe, dignified, and rewarding environment is crucial for achieving well-being. Nussbaum, meanwhile, provides a list of central human capabilities, including bodily health, emotions, and affiliation, which are directly impacted by labor conditions. Their approach challenges policymakers to view labor rights as essential for the holistic development of individuals and the overall flourishing of society.

The intersectionality of labor rights, as explored through feminist and critical race theories, further deepens the analysis by revealing how labor injustices often intersect with other forms of social oppression. These perspectives challenge traditional labor rights frameworks to more comprehensively address issues such as gender and racial disparities in the workplace. They call for a holistic approach to labor rights that is attentive to the diverse experiences and challenges faced by different demographic groups, advocating for systemic changes that promote inclusivity and fairness.

Feminist critiques underscore how gendered labor practices, such as wage disparities and the undervaluation of caregiving work, perpetuate economic inequality. Critical race theorists emphasize that systemic racism often leaves minority workers at a distinct disadvantage in terms of job opportunities, wages, and working conditions. By incorporating these insights, labor rights advocacy must extend beyond conventional demands to address the structural inequities that undermine the rights of marginalized groups.

In synthesizing these rich philosophical insights, the discourse on workers' rights emerges as a compelling narrative of ethical and social reform. This narrative challenges contemporary societies to critically assess and reconfigure labor practices to better align with fundamental human rights and dignity. Marx's focus on alienation, Mill's emphasis on autonomy, and Sen and Nussbaum's capabilities approach collectively frame labor rights as essential for cultivating a society where work enriches life rather than diminishes it.

As we explore the ongoing challenges and transformative potential of labor rights in contemporary settings, these philosophical underpinnings guide our pursuit of equitable and humane labor policies. In a globalized economy marked by precarious work and technological disruptions, these foundational ideas compel us to craft labor practices that prioritize human well-being, promote social justice, and ensure that work remains a path to empowerment rather than exploitation.

Contemporary Challenges and Inequities in Labor

In today's global economy, the landscape of labor is marked by profound transformations that challenge traditional notions of work and worker rights. The emergence of the gig economy, the pervasive impact of automation, and the complexities introduced by globalization are reshaping the very fabric of labor relations. These developments necessitate a deep philosophical reconsideration of labor rights, integrating nuanced discussions of equity, justice, and human dignity into the contemporary labor discourse.

The gig economy, a paradigm shift in traditional employment, epitomizes flexibility and independence but often at the cost of security and stability. This sector frequently circumvents the established frameworks of labor protection, leaving workers without the safeguards of stable income, health benefits, or pensions. The precarious nature of such work challenges the ethical foundations of labor rights, juxtaposing the autonomy of flexible work against the instability and vulnerability it engenders. This dichotomy raises critical questions about the balance of freedoms in the gig economy: the freedom from rigid work schedules versus the freedom from financial precarity.

Further complicating the labor landscape is the relentless march of automation. Technological advancements promise efficiency and growth but also pose existential threats to traditional employment. The displacement of workers by machines is not merely an economic issue but a profound ethical dilemma. It challenges societies to redefine the value of human labor beyond economic metrics, considering the broader implications for personal identity and social cohesion. The rapid pace of automation demands a philosophical inquiry into the nature of work itself: What roles can, or should human beings play in an automated world? How do we balance technological progress with the need to preserve meaningful employment?

Globalization introduces another layer of complexity, extending the reach of labor markets across borders but often exacerbating inequalities between the developed and developing worlds. The ethical implications are significant—multinational corporations may benefit from the lower labor costs in less developed regions, but this often comes at the expense of workers' rights and working conditions. The global supply chain thus becomes a focal point for ethical scrutiny, prompting questions about the responsibilities of those who control capital and the rights of those who provide labor. The concept of justice is stretched across international boundaries, challenging global and local policymakers to forge agreements that uphold dignified labor standards universally.

These contemporary challenges intersect with broader societal issues, disproportionately affecting vulnerable populations, including minorities, women, and the economically disadvantaged. This intersectionality underscores the multifaceted nature of labor injustices, necessitating comprehensive policy responses that address both economic and social dimensions. Such policies must consider not only the direct impacts of labor market changes but also the subtler effects on social inequality and individual well-being.

Addressing these multifaceted challenges requires an innovative approach to labor rights that is responsive to the changing dynamics of work. This involves not only adapting existing legal frameworks to cover new forms of employment but also proactively designing policies that can preempt and mitigate the adverse effects of these transformations. Philosophically, this approach draws upon a rich tradition of thought that values human labor not just as an economic activity but as a key component of human dignity and social justice.

In crafting future labor policies, integrating philosophical insights with empirical data becomes crucial. By grounding policy decisions in a deep understanding of both the practical and ethical dimensions of labor, societies can strive to create labor markets that are not only efficient but also equitable. This commitment to upholding the dignity of work in all its forms is essential for ensuring that progress in labor markets translates into progress in human development and social equity.

Policy Solutions and Global Movements

In the contemporary landscape where the dynamics of labor are continuously evolving, the discourse surrounding workers' rights demands a sophisticated integration of theoretical rigor and empirical analysis. This discourse spans the local to the global, threading through the intricacies of policy frameworks and the fabric of international labor standards, all within the broader context of a globalized economy.

The push for progressive labor policies such as living wage laws reflects a paradigm shift in how societies value labor beyond mere economic metrics. Living wage initiatives, which aim to anchor wages to the actual costs of living, do more than provide economic relief; they articulate a societal commitment to human dignity. This policy intervention represents an ethical stance, asserting that all labor should provide a means to live a dignified and fulfilling life, thereby redefining the moral imperatives of market economies.

Health and safety regulations are similarly imbued with ethical considerations, addressing the physical and psychological well-being of workers. These regulations challenge the traditional profit-driven motives of industrial production, advocating instead for a balance where worker safety is not sacrificed at the altar of productivity. Such policies underscore the principle that the well-being of workers is integral, not ancillary, to the health of the economy. They manifest a recognition that safeguarding workers' health directly impacts societal health, thus broadening the scope of these regulations beyond individual workplaces to encompass public health and safety.

In the context of the gig economy, the conventional frameworks of labor rights are often inadequate, necessitating innovative legal responses. This sector, characterized by its flexible yet precarious nature, exposes the shortcomings of traditional labor laws that do not account for non-standard work arrangements. Enhanced protections for gig workers, therefore, must creatively extend the scope of labor rights to encompass the realities of modern employment landscapes. These adaptations are not merely reactive but proactive, anticipating the evolving nature of work and ensuring that flexibility does not undermine fundamental rights.

Internationally, the role of organizations such as the International Labour Organization (ILO) is critical in harmonizing labor standards across borders. The ILO's framework for international labor standards offers a blueprint for countries to model their labor laws, promoting a baseline of decency and fairness in labor practices worldwide. The global standards set by the ILO facilitate a unified approach to labor rights, ensuring that economic globalization does not lead to a downward spiral of working conditions. This international collaboration is essential in an era where multinational corporations operate across multiple jurisdictions, potentially exploiting disparities in labor standards.

Moreover, the global movements for workers' rights illustrate the power of transnational advocacy networks and solidarity. These movements, often spearheaded by coalitions of labor unions, NGOs, and social activists, have successfully pressured both governments and international bodies to adopt and enforce more stringent labor protections. Examples from various countries, where grassroots activism has led to significant labor reforms, highlight the efficacy of sustained advocacy and strategic international alliances. These case studies not only serve as proof of concept but also as beacons of hope and instruction for ongoing and future labor rights campaigns.

In synthesizing these complex elements, the discourse on workers' rights reveals a rich tapestry of ethical, economic, and political threads. Each policy initiative, international standard, or advocacy movement is a reflection of deeper philosophical commitments to justice, equity, and human dignity. As we navigate the challenges and opportunities presented by the changing nature of work, these philosophical underpinnings provide the critical lens through which to assess and advance the agenda for workers' rights.

The integration of sophisticated policy analysis with robust philosophical inquiry in this exploration ensures a comprehensive understanding of the contemporary and future landscape of labor rights. This approach not only addresses the intellectual demands of the topic but also provides a pragmatic roadmap for actualizing the rights of workers in an increasingly complex global economy.

Conclusion

The conclusion of this discourse on workers' rights encapsulates a profound philosophical and practical exploration, intertwining theories from Marx, Mill, Sen, and Nussbaum with contemporary labor challenges. This rich dialogue not only illuminates the diverse philosophical perspectives but also delves into the urgent practical considerations necessary to address the evolving landscape of labor. The synthesis of these elements accentuates the imperative role of workers' rights in sculpting a just society—an endeavor that necessitates relentless advocacy, innovative policymaking, and robust global cooperation.

The philosophical underpinnings provided by Karl Marx introduce a critical perspective on the capitalist framework, highlighting labor not merely as a commodity but as an intrinsic aspect of human existence and self-actualization. Marx's analysis of alienation and exploitation lays bare the dehumanizing potential of labor systems that prioritize profit over people. This foundational critique challenges us to reconsider the structure of labor relations, advocating for a reorganization that ensures workers are not merely tools of production but valued participants in economic processes.

Complementing Marx, John Stuart Mill's liberal philosophy injects a nuanced discussion of individual liberties within the labor context. Mill champions the protection of personal freedoms, underscoring the importance of safeguarding autonomy in the workplace to uphold a broader democratic ethos. His advocacy for workers' rights extends beyond economic considerations, emphasizing that true liberty includes the freedom to work in conditions that respect human dignity and foster individual well-being.

Amartya Sen and Martha Nussbaum's capabilities approach further enriches this discussion by shifting the focus toward what individuals are able to achieve through work. This perspective highlights the role of employment in enhancing personal capabilities and, by extension, in enabling individuals to lead lives they value. From this vantage point, workers' rights are seen as crucial mechanisms for expanding human capabilities, thereby contributing to overall societal progress and equity.

Moreover, the incorporation of intersectional analyses into the discourse on labor rights reveals how deeply labor injustices are entwined with other forms of social and economic disparities. Issues of gender, race, and global inequality are brought to the forefront, illustrating how the struggle for labor rights is inextricably linked to broader fights against oppression. This complex interplay demands a holistic approach to labor rights that not only rectifies injustices but also fosters an inclusive environment where all workers can thrive.

The philosophical richness of the discussion on workers' rights provides a robust ethical framework for addressing the contemporary challenges faced by workers globally. These challenges, manifested in the gig economy, automation, and globalization, underscore the need for adaptive and forward-looking labor policies. Such policies must not only mitigate the adverse effects of economic transformations but also leverage these changes to enhance worker empowerment and equity.

Innovative policymaking is thus pivotal in this context. Policies that extend labor protections to gig economy workers, which address the implications of automation on employment, and that ensure fair labor standards in a globalized economy are essential. Each policy initiative should be informed by the philosophical principles discussed, ensuring that they not only respond to immediate labor market needs but also adhere to broader ethical imperatives.

Global cooperation is equally critical in the realm of labor rights. As labor issues increasingly transcend national borders, international collaboration becomes indispensable in establishing and enforcing standards that protect workers everywhere. Organizations like the International Labour Organization play a vital role in this regard, facilitating dialogue and coordination among nations to uphold dignified and fair working conditions worldwide.

Reflecting on the critical importance of workers' rights in achieving a just society, it is evident that these rights are foundational to social justice. They ensure that economic progress does not come at the cost of human dignity and equity. The ongoing advocacy for workers' rights—supported by philosophical rigor and practical action—remains a moral imperative. It is essential not only for the welfare of individual workers but for the health of societies at large.

As this chapter concludes, the call for continued engagement and persistent efforts to enhance workers' rights is clear. The path forward requires a concerted effort from all stakeholders—governments, businesses, and civil societies—to ensure that the labor market continues to evolve in ways that respect and promote the intrinsic value of work and the rights of those who perform it.

CHAPTER 5
EDUCATING FOR EQUITY

Education stands as a profound cornerstone of society, not merely facilitating the transfer of knowledge but also shaping the cultural and ethical fabric of communities. It is at the educational crossroads where individual potential meets societal expectations, where personal growth is intertwined with collective advancement. Thus, the philosophy of education, particularly its role in fostering equity, deserves meticulous scrutiny and deliberate discourse. This chapter delves deep into how educational systems can be reformed to promote not only equity but also to dismantle the economic barriers that perpetuate cycles of inequality. It is an exploration that is as much about philosophical orientation as it is about pragmatic concerns, acknowledging that education is both a fundamental human right and a pivotal battleground for social justice.

The essence of educational equity transcends the simplistic goal of uniform resource allocation to address the nuanced needs of diverse student populations. Rooted in a rich tapestry of philosophical thought, the quest for equity in education challenges us to rethink the purposes and approaches of our educational institutions. It compels us to consider not just the accessibility of education but its capability to empower and elevate, to transform lives in meaningful ways that resonate beyond classroom walls. Educational equity is anchored in the belief that every individual, regardless of their socio-economic background, race, or geographical location, deserves access to high-quality education that nurtures their potential and respects their inherent dignity.

Historically, philosophers like John Dewey have underscored the transformative power of education. Dewey viewed education as an essential mechanism for social change and personal development, arguing that learning should be active and engaging, fostering a sense of curiosity and critical thinking. According to Dewey, education is not a preparation for life but life itself; it is a continuous reconstruction of experiences that enlarges and integrates individuals within their societies. This vision champions a pedagogy that is responsive to the needs of all students, one that equips them to navigate and influence the world around them positively.

In parallel, Paulo Freire's critique of traditional pedagogies—which he saw as oppressive and stifling—introduces another layer to our understanding of educational equity. Freire advocated for a "problem-posing" education, a dynamic method where students and teachers engage in dialogue, reflecting critically on their realities and, through this process, become empowered to challenge and change them. His philosophy reveals the deep connections between education, identity, and power, illuminating how educational practices can either reinforce societal inequities or help dismantle them. Freire's work encourages us to view education as an act of liberation, a critical tool for social justice that encourages students to question and transform the structures that marginalize some while privileging others.

The need for educational equity is further magnified by the persistent disparities evident across global educational landscapes. These disparities are not merely academic but are indicative of broader social and economic inequalities that educational systems can perpetuate or alleviate. The challenge, therefore, is to reconfigure these systems in ways that genuinely level the playing field. This involves integrating technology to bridge learning gaps, redesigning curricula that reflect diverse cultural perspectives, and ensuring that educational policies are not only inclusive but also actively anti-discriminatory.

Moreover, the role of educators in this transformative process is pivotal. Teachers are not just conveyors of knowledge but also architects of student experiences and agents of change within their communities. Their ability to mold educational environments that are inclusive, engaging, and enlightening is crucial for the realization of educational equity. This task, however, is complex and requires a robust support system that includes continuous professional development, adequate resources, and a school culture that values diversity and inclusivity.

As we embark on this exploration of the philosophy of education and its implications for equity, we must recognize the enormity of the task at hand. Reforming educational systems to promote equity involves a multifaceted approach that challenges existing paradigms and calls for a concerted effort among policymakers, educators, and communities. It demands innovative thinking, persistent advocacy, and a relentless commitment to social justice.

In synthesizing the philosophical underpinnings with practical considerations, this chapter sets the stage for a deeper examination of how education can serve as a powerful catalyst for social equity. It highlights the necessity of viewing educational reform not just as a policy challenge but as a moral imperative, urging us to re-envision education as a tool for leveling societal imbalances and cultivating a more just and equitable world.

This introduction endeavors to weave together the philosophical and the practical, presenting a compelling narrative that underscores the critical importance of educational equity in achieving a just society. Through this lens, we will explore the transformative potential of education in subsequent sections, analyzing both the philosophical depth and the practical breadth of this crucial issue.

Philosophical Underpinnings of Educational Equity

In the vast landscape of educational philosophy, the pursuit of equity intertwines deeply with ethical inquiries about the purpose of education and its role in shaping a just society. This exploration goes beyond mere access and resource allocation, questioning the fundamental aims of educational systems and their capacity to cultivate individuals equipped to challenge and reshape societal norms. This complex web of philosophical thought draws from a diverse array of scholars, each providing unique insights that collectively enrich our understanding of what it means to educate for equity.

At the core of this philosophical journey is the existential and ethical consideration of education as a transformative force in human life. Education, in its ideal form, is posited not only as a mechanism for transmitting knowledge but as a profound means of personal and communal transformation. This transformative vision of education is articulated by philosophers such as John Dewey, who envisages education as a living process through which individuals continuously recreate themselves and their worlds. Dewey's progressive education theory emphasizes experiential learning, where students engage with their environment in ways that foster practical problem-solving skills and democratic cooperation. According to Dewey, the school is not just an institution for book learning but a social institution where students learn the value of community and collective responsibility.

Expanding on Dewey's vision, Paulo Freire's critical pedagogy introduces a radical critique of traditional education systems that he describes as "banking" models—where students are passive recipients of deposited knowledge. Freire argues for a dialogic model of education that recognizes students as co-creators of knowledge. His approach emphasizes the importance of consciousness-raising, where education becomes a practice of freedom that helps individuals identify and challenge oppressive social structures. For Freire, educational equity is deeply linked to social emancipation; it involves empowering individuals to perceive social, political, and economic contradictions and to take action against oppressive elements of reality.

The philosophical discourse also draws significantly from the capabilities approach, developed by Amartya Sen and furthered by Martha Nussbaum, which shifts the focus from mere access to educational resources to what individuals are able to do and to become as a result of their education. This approach advocates for an education that enhances essential human capabilities, such as the ability to engage in economic transactions, participate in political decisions, and live with dignity in the face of moral and practical choices. Sen and Nussbaum argue that educational equity requires not only equipping individuals with competencies but also enabling them to pursue a range of valuable life paths. This perspective frames education as a key element in expanding personal and collective agency, emphasizing its role in cultivating a more reflective, critical, and dynamically capable citizenry.

Integrating these philosophical insights, the discussion on educational equity also confronts the practical realities of implementing such transformative educational principles in diverse sociopolitical contexts. The challenge is not only philosophical but deeply pragmatic, involving the design and enactment of educational policies and practices that align with these rich ethical imperatives. It requires a nuanced understanding of local and global educational disparities and a committed effort to tailor educational reforms that genuinely address the specific needs and potentials of diverse student populations.

Furthermore, the global dimension of educational equity cannot be overlooked. In an increasingly interconnected world, the philosophy of education must grapple with global injustices and strive to foster an international ethos of mutual respect and understanding. This includes preparing students not only to succeed in their local communities but also to engage responsibly and compassionately on the global stage.

In this light, educational equity emerges as a complex, multidimensional endeavor that requires ongoing critical examination and robust philosophical grounding. It challenges educators, policymakers, and scholars to persistently advocate for reforms that are both reflective of and responsive to the changing needs of a global society. As we delve into specific proposals for educational reform, these philosophical underpinnings serve as a guide, helping to ensure that efforts to promote educational equity are deeply informed by a commitment to justice, empowerment, and the dignity of all individuals.

This robust philosophical foundation provides a unique perspective on educating for equity, emphasizing its critical importance in achieving a just society and highlighting the need for continuous advocacy, innovative policymaking, and extensive global cooperation to realize these ideals effectively.

Proposals for Educational Reform

Reforming education to dismantle social and economic barriers entails a comprehensive reevaluation of existing policies and the introduction of transformative measures that align with philosophical imperatives for justice and equity. The process involves multifaceted strategies, including equitable funding models, the integration of technology, and curricular reforms that promote inclusivity and critical thinking. Each of these areas demands active participation from policymakers, educators, and communities to effectively address the nuances of implementation and the wide-ranging impacts of these reforms.

One of the foundational reforms in the pursuit of educational equity is the development and implementation of equitable funding models. Traditional funding mechanisms often exacerbate disparities by allocating resources based on local property taxes, leading to well-funded schools in affluent areas and under-resourced schools in poorer districts. An equitable funding model, conversely, aims to level the educational playing field by ensuring that all schools receive funding based on the specific needs of their students. This approach not only addresses disparities in educational quality between affluent and poorer areas but also considers factors such as the number of students who need additional support, including those with disabilities, English language learners, and students from economically disadvantaged backgrounds. By adjusting funding based on specific educational needs rather than property values, systems can move closer to providing every student with an equal opportunity to succeed.

Moreover, the integration of technology in education has emerged as a crucial strategy for bridging learning gaps and enhancing access to quality education. In an era where digital tools and resources proliferate, technology can play a transformative role in personalizing learning experiences and providing real-time feedback that helps students improve. However, the integration of technology must be thoughtfully managed to avoid new forms of inequity, such as the digital divide that leaves students in low-income areas without access to necessary technological tools. Effective policy interventions must therefore ensure not only the availability of technology but also its accessibility to all students, coupled with teacher training that enables educators to integrate digital tools effectively into their teaching practices.

Curricular reforms are equally vital in promoting a more inclusive, equitable, and relevant education. An inclusive curriculum reflects and respects the diverse cultural backgrounds of all students, providing them with mirrors to see themselves and windows to view others. Such curricular reforms encourage the incorporation of diverse perspectives and foster an environment where students learn to appreciate and critically engage with a variety of cultural and historical viewpoints. Furthermore, emphasizing critical thinking within the curriculum prepares students to analyze and challenge existing societal structures, equipping them with the skills necessary to become agents of change in their own lives and in their communities.

The role of policymakers in these reforms is to provide the vision, legislative framework, and resources necessary to drive change. They must work closely with educational experts to design policies that address systemic inequities and to ensure that reforms are responsive to the evolving educational landscape. Educators, on the other hand, are on the frontline of implementing these reforms. Their involvement in the policy-making process is critical, as they bring practical insights that can inform more effective and applicable educational strategies. Additionally, educators' commitment to professional development and adaptability plays a crucial role in the successful integration of new teaching methods and technologies.

Communities also have a pivotal role in the educational reform process. Engaged communities can advocate for necessary changes and support the implementation of new policies through various forms of participation and support. Community involvement ensures that educational reforms are grounded in the real-world needs and expectations of those they aim to serve, providing a check against top-down initiatives that may not align with local needs.

The potential impacts of these changes on both a national and global scale are profound. Nationally, educational reforms can lead to a more equitable society by leveling the educational playing field, reducing dropout rates, and increasing college readiness among historically underserved populations. Globally, the exchange of ideas and best practices for educational equity can inspire international reforms, fostering a generation of globally minded citizens who are well-equipped to tackle the challenges of an interconnected world.

As we contemplate these extensive reforms, it is evident that the journey toward educational equity is complex and fraught with challenges. However, the philosophical commitment to justice and the practical pursuit of reform provides a dual framework for action that holds the promise of transforming education into a true engine of equity and social change.

Conclusion

We must distill the essence of philosophical discussions and practical applications explored in this chapter to underscore the transformative power of education as an equitable force within society. This discourse has woven through the conceptual fabric of philosophical thought leaders, merging seamlessly with modern calls for systemic change in the educational landscape. Here, we will reflect on the inherent importance of persistently advocating for educational reforms that promote equity, emphasizing the crucial role of collaborative policymaking and innovative practices.

Education, when understood through the lens of philosophers like Dewey and Freire and contemporary advocates like Sen and Nussbaum, emerges not just as a tool for personal enrichment but as a profound societal lever for justice and equality. These philosophical frameworks provide a robust foundation for rethinking educational systems and their role in mitigating social and economic disparities. Dewey's emphasis on experiential learning underscores the importance of engaging students in education that mirrors the complexities of real life, fostering critical thinking and democratic participation. Freire's critical pedagogy, with its focus on dialogue and reflection, challenges oppressive structures within traditional education systems and empowers students to transform their own realities.

The capabilities approach introduced by Sen and expanded by Nussbaum shifts our focus from traditional academic outcomes to a broader spectrum of human development. This perspective advocates for an education system that does more than fill students with knowledge; it strives to build environments that enable individuals to pursue a spectrum of valued life paths. This approach not only amplifies the importance of access to quality education but also stresses the variety of capabilities that education should foster—from critical thinking and emotional development to practical skills that align with evolving global demands.

Addressing the role of policymakers, educators, and communities in implementing these reforms, it is evident that a multifaceted approach is required. Policymakers must craft legislation that embodies these philosophical insights, translating lofty ideals into actionable, grounded policies that address the nuances of local and global educational challenges. This involves not only reallocating resources to ensure equitable access across diverse populations but also redefining educational standards and outcomes in ways that reflect a commitment to holistic development.

Educators, for their part, are tasked with the practical application of these policies within the classroom. Their role is pivotal—they are the interpreters and implementers of educational reforms, acting as the bridge between policy and practice. For educators, embracing these philosophical perspectives means fostering an environment where students are encouraged to question, explore, and contribute, effectively preparing them to participate in a democratic society.

Communities also play a critical role, serving as both beneficiaries and informants of educational policy. Community engagement in educational reform ensures that policies are responsive to the unique cultural, economic, and social needs of diverse populations. Moreover, communities can hold educational systems accountable, ensuring that they continue to strive for equity and excellence in practice, not just in theory.

Reflecting on the global implications of these reforms, it becomes clear that the quest for educational equity is not confined by national borders. In an interconnected world, the challenges and solutions in education have international repercussions. Sharing best practices, fostering international collaborations, and maintaining a global dialogue on educational reform are essential for driving worldwide progress toward equity.

In sum, the advocacy for continual reform in education is rooted in a deep philosophical commitment to justice, equity, and human dignity. It requires persistent effort, innovative thinking, and collaborative governance to ensure that education fulfills its role as a cornerstone of a just and equitable society. As we move forward, let us carry the insights from this chapter as a guide for action, inspiring all stakeholders to champion the cause of educational equity with renewed vigor and vision. This is not merely an academic or political challenge—it is a moral imperative to cultivate an enlightened, just, and equitable global society.

CHAPTER 6
THE FIGHT FOR CIVIL RIGHTS

The struggle for civil rights, historically rooted in the quest for racial equality in the mid-20th century, has undergone profound transformations, expanded its reach and reshaping its agendas to confront an array of injustices that permeate modern society. Initially galvanized by the courage of figures like Martin Luther King Jr. and Rosa Parks, who fought against the blight of segregation and discrimination, the movement has evolved to address not only racial injustice but also disparities in gender, sexual orientation, and beyond. This evolution reflects a dynamic and responsive civil rights movement that adapts to the shifting landscapes of social injustice, highlighting the enduring need for reforms that are deeply informed by moral philosophy.

In its inception, the civil rights movement was primarily a response to the systemic inequities faced by African Americans in the United States. It sought to dismantle the institutional barriers of Jim Crow laws and widespread discriminatory practices that denied African Americans their fundamental rights and freedoms. The landmark achievements of this era, including the Civil Rights Act of 1964 and the Voting Rights Act of 1965, were monumental, not only in their immediate impact but in setting a precedent for legal and social reform.

As the movement has matured, its focus has broadened, drawing in a diverse coalition of activists and advocates from various backgrounds. This expansion has seen the civil rights discourse embracing issues of gender equality, championed by the women's rights movement, which has fought tirelessly against the systemic sexism and inequality that pervade aspects of society from the workplace to personal autonomy. Similarly, the LGBTQ+ rights movement has gained momentum, challenging laws and norms that discriminate against individuals based on their sexual orientation or gender identity. These efforts underscore a fundamental shift in the scope of civil rights, reflecting a comprehensive approach to combating all forms of discrimination.

Today, the civil rights movement faces a landscape marked by both old challenges and new. Racial injustice remains a pervasive issue, as evidenced by police brutality and the disproportionate incarceration rates among African American communities. These enduring issues are compounded by emergent challenges such as digital privacy concerns, economic inequality, and environmental justice, which disproportionately affect marginalized populations. These multifaceted challenges demand a reinvigorated approach to civil rights advocacy—one that is deeply grounded in moral philosophy.

The central thesis of this chapter, therefore, posits that contemporary civil rights issues necessitate a robust approach informed by ethical considerations of equity, justice, and human dignity. The moral imperatives guiding this discourse draw upon a rich philosophical foundation that views each individual as deserving of respect and justice irrespective of their race, gender, sexual orientation, or socio-economic status. This approach not only seeks to rectify historical injustices but also to proactively shape a society that upholds the dignity of all its members against emerging forms of discrimination and inequality.

Grounding civil rights advocacy in moral philosophy involves revisiting the ethical principles that underscore the value of each human life and the rights inherent to all individuals. Philosophers such as John Rawls have contributed significantly to this discourse, with theories that emphasize fairness and the equitable distribution of resources as foundational to a just society. Similarly, contemporary thinkers continue to explore how justice can be achieved in diverse societies with complex, overlapping identities and how rights can be extended to ensure not just freedom from discrimination but the active participation of all in the civic life of their communities.

In essence, the fight for civil rights, while evolving, remains a pivotal testament to society's capacity to reflect upon and reformulate its moral and legal frameworks. As we delve deeper into the specific contemporary issues and the proposed reforms in subsequent discussions, it is crucial to keep these ethical imperatives at the forefront, guiding our exploration and actions. This commitment to justice, equity, and human dignity is not merely theoretical but a practical imperative that drives the continuous and necessary evolution of the civil rights movement today. This evolving fight, rooted in a deep-seated belief in equality and fairness, challenges us to envision and strive for a society where justice is not an ideal but a reality for all.

Analyzing Contemporary Civil Rights Issues

The landscape of contemporary civil rights issues is both vast and complex, marked by persistent systemic inequities and emergent challenges that demand rigorous scrutiny and decisive action. Today, these issues manifest in numerous forms, from entrenched systemic racism and police brutality to gender discrimination and disparities in the criminal justice system. Each of these issues profoundly impacts affected communities, not only undermining their rights and dignity but also perpetuating cycles of disadvantage and oppression that ripple through generations.

Systemic racism, a deeply ingrained issue, continues to manifest through various societal structures, affecting everything from education and employment to housing and healthcare. African American communities, in particular, face disproportionate challenges, with racism embedded in the very fabric of daily interactions and institutional operations. This systemic issue extends to the realm of police brutality, where racial profiling and disproportionate use of force against people of color have sparked national and international outrage. The deaths of individuals like George Floyd and Breonna Taylor are not isolated incidents but stark representations of widespread and enduring racial injustices that catalyze the civil rights movements of today.

In the criminal justice system, disparities manifest in sentencing, incarceration rates, and the treatment of prisoners. People of color, particularly African Americans and Latinos, are disproportionately represented in prison populations and are more likely to receive harsher sentences than their white counterparts for similar offenses. This systemic bias not only affects the individuals incarcerated but also has a devastating impact on their families and communities, perpetuating cycles of poverty, disenfranchisement, and social marginalization.

Discrimination based on gender and sexual orientation also presents significant civil rights challenges. Despite advances in some areas, women continue to face systemic barriers in the workforce, including wage disparities and limited advancement opportunities, compounded by instances of harassment and discrimination. The #MeToo movement has played a critical role in bringing these issues to light, catalyzing a global dialogue about sexual harassment and gender discrimination, not only in workplaces but in all areas of life. Similarly, the LGBTQ+ community faces ongoing discrimination, with issues ranging from rights to marriage and adoption to protections against discrimination in employment and public accommodations. In many places, transgender individuals, in particular, face acute risks and are often subjected to both systemic discrimination and individual acts of violence.

Modern movements and activism have been pivotal in highlighting these contemporary civil rights issues and pushing for significant societal and legislative changes. Movements like Black Lives Matter have galvanized public support and driven the conversation around police reform and racial justice to the forefront of political discourse. These movements use a combination of grassroots activism and digital platforms to mobilize supporters, organize demonstrations, and hold institutions accountable. They have also been instrumental in influencing policy discussions at all levels of government, advocating for comprehensive reforms such as the banning of chokeholds, the establishment of national databases of police misconduct, and the redirection of funds from policing to community-based support systems.

Similarly, the #MeToo movement has reshaped conversations around gender equality and justice, challenging societal norms and demanding changes in laws and policies that protect against gender-based violence and discrimination. This movement has highlighted the pervasive nature of sexual harassment and has empowered individuals to come forward with their stories, fostering a collective call for change that transcends national borders.

The role of these movements in civil rights advocacy illustrates a powerful response to systemic injustices, reflecting a broader trend towards more inclusive and intersectional approaches to civil rights.

These movements emphasize the importance of listening to and amplifying marginalized voices, integrating their experiences and perspectives into a broader civil rights agenda that seeks not only to remedy historical injustices but to reimagine a society in which equity and justice are accessible to all.

Reflecting on these issues and the activism that seeks to address them, it is clear that the fight for civil rights in the contemporary era is as urgent as ever. It requires a committed, sustained effort that spans multiple generations and demographics, uniting individuals across diverse backgrounds in a shared struggle for justice. The profound impacts of these civil rights challenges on affected communities call for an approach that is not only responsive but also proactive, seeking to dismantle the systemic barriers that perpetuate inequality and to construct an inclusive framework for civil rights that reflects the moral imperatives of equity, justice, and human dignity.

Advocating for Comprehensive Reforms

The urgency to address the deep-seated civil rights issues permeating our society calls for comprehensive reforms that are not only effective but ethically justified. These reforms must span multiple sectors—law enforcement, judicial systems, education, and economic structures—to ensure that they collectively foster a more equitable and just society. The moral grounding for such reforms is drawn from a variety of philosophical frameworks that emphasize justice, equality, and the intrinsic worth of every individual.

In the realm of law enforcement, reform is critical to addressing the issues of systemic racism and police brutality that have been highlighted by numerous tragic incidents and sustained public protests. One of the key reforms in this area could involve the implementation of community policing strategies, which focus on building ties and working closely with community members, thereby fostering mutual trust and respect. Additionally, policies such as the mandatory use of body cameras, the establishment of independent oversight committees with the power to investigate and prosecute instances of police misconduct, and extensive training that emphasizes de-escalation techniques and cultural competency are crucial. These changes aim not only to reduce incidents of brutality but to rebuild trust between law enforcement agencies and the communities they serve.

Judicial reforms are equally vital in ensuring that the criminal justice system becomes a true system of justice rather than one of mere punishment. This involves eliminating mandatory minimum sentences, which disproportionately affect minority communities, and reforming bail systems that penalize the poor, effectively criminalizing poverty. Expanding public defender resources to ensure that all individuals receive competent legal representation regardless of their financial status is another critical step. These reforms are rooted in the principles of justice and fairness, ensuring that the system is equitable and just for all, irrespective of socioeconomic status or racial background.

In the educational sector, promoting diversity and inclusion involves curricular reforms that integrate a wider range of perspectives and histories, particularly those of historically marginalized communities. This also includes implementing hiring practices aimed at increasing diversity among teachers and administrators, as well as policies that ensure equitable funding for schools serving disadvantaged communities. Educational reforms should also address disparities in disciplinary practices, which often disproportionately impact students of color, and support inclusive educational environments that cultivate an understanding and appreciation of diversity among all students. These changes are underpinned by the philosophical assertion that education should be a vehicle for empowerment and liberation, not oppression.

Economic reforms are necessary to address the structural inequalities that underpin many of the civil rights issues faced today. Policies aimed at reducing income inequality, such as progressive taxation, increased minimum wages, and enhanced social security nets, are critical. Furthermore, initiatives to ensure equal pay for equal work, support for affordable housing, and access to healthcare play a direct role in leveling the economic playing field. The philosophy supporting these economic reforms is largely derived from theories of distributive justice, which argue for a fair allocation of resources within society, ensuring that all individuals have the opportunities necessary to lead fulfilling lives.

The philosophical frameworks that support these reforms are varied but intersect in their commitment to justice, equality, and human dignity. John Rawls' theory of justice as fairness, for example, emphasizes that social and economic inequalities are to be arranged so that they are both reasonably expected to be to everyone's advantage, and attached to positions and offices open to all. Martha Nussbaum's capabilities approach extends this discussion by focusing on what individuals are able to do and to be, thus advocating for a society that enables all its members to develop their full potential. These theories, along with the critical insights of thinkers like Michel Foucault and Angela Davis, who explore the power dynamics and systemic structures of oppression within societies, provide a robust ethical foundation for advocating comprehensive civil rights reforms.

Ultimately, advocating for these reforms requires a collective effort—a chorus of voices demanding change, supported by philosophical convictions that assert the worth and dignity of every individual. It is a challenge that calls for persistent advocacy, innovative policymaking, and a deep commitment to the principles of equity and justice. As we push forward with these reforms, it is crucial to remember that the fight for civil rights is not only about correcting past injustices but about shaping a future that reflects our deepest values of fairness, dignity, and equality for all.

Conclusion

As we conclude our exploration of the contemporary civil rights landscape, we recognize the critical importance of understanding and addressing the myriad of injustices that continue to challenge the very fabric of our society. This chapter has traversed the terrain of systemic racism, police brutality, gender and sexual orientation discrimination, and the overarching disparities within the criminal justice system, underscoring how these profound issues are manifested and the devastating impacts they have on affected communities. Through a detailed examination of specific proposals for reform, grounded in robust moral philosophy, we envision a path forward—one that is paved with equity, justice, and human dignity.

The journey through contemporary civil rights issues has highlighted not only the enduring struggles but also the dynamic nature of activism that strives to address and adapt to these evolving challenges. The moral imperatives that drive this activism are rooted in a deep philosophical commitment to justice— as articulated by thinkers from John Rawls to Martha Nussbaum—and a recognition of the intrinsic worth of every individual. These principles compel us to advocate for systemic changes that aim not only to rectify historical injustices but also to proactively cultivate an environment where such disparities are no longer perpetuated.

Our discussions have emphasized the necessity of comprehensive reforms across various sectors of society. In law enforcement, the implementation of community policing and rigorous training programs aims to rebuild trust and ensure that police officers can serve as protectors rather than oppressors of community rights. Judicial reforms, including the elimination of mandatory minimum sentences and the overhaul of bail systems, seek to restore fairness to a system marred by biases that disproportionately impact the most vulnerable populations. Educational reforms advocate for curricula that embrace diversity and foster inclusivity, empowering students from all backgrounds to engage with and appreciate the rich tapestry of human experiences. Meanwhile, economic policies designed to reduce inequality and provide equitable opportunities for all underline the interconnectedness of civil rights with broader socioeconomic structures.

The potential impact of these proposed reforms is profound. By addressing the root causes of inequality and discrimination, these changes have the potential to transform society fundamentally. They promise not just to alleviate the symptoms of injustice but to forge a society that values and upholds the rights of all its members. This transformation is essential not only for those who suffer most acutely from civil rights violations but for the broader health of our democracy and the moral integrity of our collective community.

Yet, the realization of these reforms requires more than theoretical endorsement; it demands active and sustained engagement. Ongoing advocacy is crucial, as the path towards true equality is fraught with resistance and setbacks. Community engagement is equally vital, providing the grassroots support necessary to drive change from the bottom up. Political action, too, plays a pivotal role, as policies and laws must be enacted and enforced to ensure lasting impact.

The fight for civil rights, therefore, is far from over. It is a perpetual struggle that must evolve in response to new challenges and changing societal contexts. As we move forward, it is imperative that we maintain vigilance and resolve in our pursuit of justice. The reforms we advocate for today will shape the society of tomorrow, influencing how future generations will live, interact, and perceive the concept of rights and responsibilities.

In this relentless pursuit, let us draw strength from the knowledge that our efforts are grounded in a solid ethical foundation—one that views each human being as deserving of respect and dignity. Let us be inspired by the successes of past movements and empowered by the tools and knowledge we possess today. Above all, let us commit to a vision of society that cherishes diversity, seeks equity, and upholds the civil rights of every individual as the cornerstone of a just and equitable world. This vision is not only a reflection of our highest moral aspirations but a beacon that guides our continuous journey towards a more perfect union.

CHAPTER 7

HOUSING AS A HUMAN RIGHT

Housing, fundamentally, represents more than mere shelter; it is an essential cornerstone of human dignity and stability. Recognized internationally as a fundamental human right, the importance of housing transcends basic utility, embodying security, privacy, and the capacity to lead a life with respect and opportunity. This recognition is anchored in various international declarations, including the Universal Declaration of Human Rights, which asserts the right to adequate housing as integral to the standard of living necessary for the health and well-being of a person and their family.

The exigency of this right becomes all the more poignant when viewed through the lens of current global housing challenges. Urban centers across the world grapple with issues such as gentrification, homelessness, and persistent affordable housing crises, each presenting complex dilemmas that call for a careful melding of philosophical inquiry and practical solutions. These issues, emblematic of broader societal inequities, not only disrupt communities but also challenge the ethical foundations upon which modern societies are built. The philosophical underpinnings supporting the imperative of housing rights draw heavily on theories of justice, equity, and human rights, emphasizing that access to decent housing is not merely a commodity but a moral imperative that societies are obligated to fulfill.

Gentrification, often touted as urban renewal or development, frequently results in the displacement of lower-income families and individuals who find themselves priced out of neighborhoods they have long called home. This phenomenon raises critical ethical questions about the balance between development and displacement, and whether the benefits of revitalization are justly distributed among all residents. The philosophical critique of gentrification hinges on the principles of distributive justice, which demand fairness in how urban renewal efforts are planned and implemented. It challenges us to consider whose interests are prioritized in such developments and to seek strategies that protect vulnerable populations against the erosion of their communities.

Homelessness represents another severe manifestation of housing inequity, with millions around the world lacking stable and secure places to live. The root causes of homelessness are multifaceted, involving a tangle of economic, social, and personal factors that include unemployment, insufficient social welfare, mental health issues, and systemic failures in housing policies. Philosophically, the existence of homelessness in societies that have the means to prevent it calls into question our moral commitments to one another. It prompts a critical examination of the social contract and the responsibilities of governments to ensure that no individual lacks basic shelter. Moreover, it challenges us to redefine what it means to be a society that upholds dignity and rights for all its members, especially the most vulnerable.

Affordable housing crises further complicate the landscape, as increasing numbers of people find themselves unable to afford adequate housing without experiencing financial strain. In cities across the globe, the rising cost of living, stagnating wages, and speculative real estate markets have converged to create environments where securing housing is a constant struggle for many. Addressing this crisis involves not only economic and policy considerations but a philosophical reevaluation of how resources are allocated and accessed in our societies. The theory of social justice provides a framework here, advocating for systems that ensure all members of society have access to the essential conditions needed for a dignified life.

As we delve deeper into these critical housing issues, the chapter will explore both the philosophical rationale and the practical measures necessary to address the challenges of gentrification, homelessness, and affordable housing shortages. By integrating ethical considerations with actionable strategies, the aim is to highlight how deeply interconnected our rights, responsibilities, and realities are when it comes to the fundamental human need for housing.

This examination sets the stage for a nuanced discussion that not only critiques the current state of housing rights but also seeks to envision and enact a future where these rights are not aspirational but actualized. The goal is to foster a society where every individual's right to housing is recognized and respected, paving the way for more equitable, just, and humane urban environments. This commitment to housing as a human right requires a robust dialogue between theory and practice, urging continuous advocacy and innovative policymaking to transform how housing is viewed and provided in our global society.

Philosophical Foundations of Housing Rights

The assertion that housing is a fundamental human right is underpinned by a rich tapestry of philosophical arguments that speak to the essence of social justice, human dignity, and the role of the state in nurturing the welfare of its citizens. These arguments are not merely abstract principles but serve as the ethical backbone for policies aimed at ensuring everyone has access to safe, affordable, and stable housing. The philosophical exploration of housing rights entails dissecting theories from the realms of ethics, political philosophy, and human rights, each providing insights into why housing must be more than an economic commodity—it must be a guaranteed right.

Central to the philosophical discussion on housing rights is the concept of human dignity. From this perspective, the ability to secure a safe and stable living environment is not a privilege but a fundamental aspect of preserving human dignity. Immanuel Kant's imperative that humanity must always be treated as an end in itself, never merely as a means, resonates deeply within this context. Housing instability and homelessness represent a failure to honor this moral principle, reducing individuals to mere survival mode, stripping them of their agency, and preventing them from fully participating in society. The dignity argument asserts that without the security of a place to call home, it is exceedingly difficult for individuals to contribute to their community or to pursue personal development and well-being.

Expanding from individual dignity to societal equity, the theories of social justice provide a broader framework for considering housing rights. John Rawls, in his seminal work "A Theory of Justice," proposes principles of justice that can be applied to housing equity. Rawls' first principle, which asserts that each person has an equal right to the most extensive basic liberties compatible with similar liberties for others, supports the notion that a just society must facilitate access to essential needs, including housing. His second principle involves arranging social and economic inequalities so that they are both to the greatest benefit of the least advantaged and attached to offices and positions open to all under conditions of fair equality of opportunity. Applied to housing, this principle supports policies that ensure even the most disadvantaged have adequate housing, as this is crucial for their chances at a fruitful life and for maintaining social stability and justice.

Furthermore, the role of the state in ensuring the welfare of its citizens is another critical area of philosophical inquiry. Philosophers such as Thomas Hobbes and John Locke discussed the social contract as a formative idea for modern states, where individuals consent to give up certain freedoms and submit to the authority of the state in return for protection of their fundamental rights. In this framework, it is the duty of the state to protect and provide for the basic needs of its citizens, including housing. If the state fails to secure this right, it is not fulfilling its end of the social contract, which can justify citizens' demands for reform and even disobedience to rectify the breach.

This philosophical exploration naturally extends to the moral obligations of society to provide housing and combat housing insecurity. From a utilitarian perspective, providing universal access to affordable housing maximizes overall happiness and utility by reducing stress, health problems, and social discontent that arise from housing precarity. The capability approach, articulated by Martha Nussbaum and Amartya Sen, also contributes to this discussion by emphasizing the role of housing in enabling individuals to perform various 'functionings' necessary to lead a life of value. Nussbaum specifically lists "bodily health" and "emotions" as central human capabilities that are directly affected by housing stability.

The synthesis of these philosophical views shapes our understanding of housing as a right and enriches the discourse on how societies should approach housing insecurity. Each perspective, whether grounded in dignity, justice, or state responsibility, converges on the conclusion that housing is not just another need but a prerequisite for a dignified, equitable, and fulfilling life. As such, it is imperative that societies, through collective action and enlightened policy making, ensure that the right to housing is not only recognized but fully realized. This philosophical foundation thus provides the moral clarity and impetus needed to advocate for and implement comprehensive housing reforms that aim to secure a stable and dignified living environment for all individuals.

Contemporary Challenges in Housing

The landscape of contemporary housing issues presents a complex tapestry of challenges that significantly impact community structures and individual lives. Among these, gentrification and homelessness stand out as particularly pervasive problems that not only reflect but also exacerbate existing inequalities within urban environments.

Gentrification, a process characterized by the influx of wealthier individuals into economically disadvantaged neighborhoods, leads to increased property values and living costs, which can displace long-standing, lower-income residents. This phenomenon often reshapes communities, resulting in a cultural shift and sometimes even a complete restructuring of neighborhood identities. The benefits of gentrification, such as revitalized infrastructure and increased economic activity, are frequently overshadowed by the displacement of vulnerable populations who find themselves priced out of their own communities without adequate affordable housing alternatives. This displacement can lead to significant disruptions in social networks that are vital for the communal support many depend upon, especially in marginalized communities.

Moreover, the ripple effects of gentrification feed into the broader issue of homelessness, a stark manifestation of housing insecurity. Homelessness is a multifaceted crisis, influenced by a combination of systemic factors—such as inadequate housing policies, lack of affordable housing, and insufficient social services—and individual circumstances, including job loss, mental health issues, and substance abuse. The visibility of homelessness in urban centers underscores the acute failures of societal safety nets to protect the most vulnerable. Homelessness not only deprives individuals of physical shelter but also of security, privacy, and dignity, further alienating them from society and perpetuating a cycle of poverty and exclusion.

Addressing these issues requires a multidimensional approach, encompassing both policy interventions and community-led initiatives. One potential solution to the challenge of gentrification involves implementing policies that ensure a percentage of new housing developments are reserved for affordable housing. This can help maintain the socio-economic diversity of neighborhoods undergoing redevelopment and provide stability for existing residents. Additionally, strengthening rent control laws can protect tenants from sudden rent hikes that lead to displacement. These measures, however, must be carefully calibrated to avoid discouraging new development altogether, which is also necessary for urban growth and vitality.

Innovative housing models present another avenue for addressing housing challenges. Cooperative housing, for example, offers residents ownership interests in their housing complexes, empowering communities and providing more stability than traditional rental arrangements. This model not only fosters a community-oriented environment but also keeps housing affordable as members are the shareholders of their own homes. Furthermore, the expansion of public housing options can provide a reliable safety net for those affected by homelessness and displacement. Public housing needs to be well-managed and sufficiently funded to ensure it serves as a viable long-term solution rather than a neglected last resort.

Community-led initiatives are crucial in this context as well. These can include local non-profits working to support affordable housing projects or grassroots movements advocating for policy changes. Community engagement ensures that the voices of those most affected by housing issues are heard in the policymaking process, increasing the relevance and effectiveness of the solutions implemented.

Looking forward, the future of housing policy must continue to innovate and adapt to the changing dynamics of urban development and population needs. It is clear that no single solution can address the breadth of housing challenges, and a combination of approaches is necessary. Ongoing activism and public engagement play pivotal roles in this effort, pushing for continuous reform and ensuring that housing policies evolve to meet the needs of all citizens. Moreover, international cooperation can offer valuable insights and best practices, as global urbanization trends suggest that housing challenges are not confined to any one region but are a widespread concern.

Tackling contemporary housing issues such as gentrification and homelessness requires a concerted effort from all levels of government, supported by active community participation and innovative policy making. By combining preventative measures with responsive solutions, it is possible to mitigate the impacts of these issues and move closer to the goal of securing housing for all, ensuring that urban environments remain diverse, vibrant, and inclusive.

The Role of Government and Policy in Securing Housing for All

The role of government in securing housing as a fundamental human right underscores a critical intersection of policy, responsibility, and moral imperative. This responsibility spans various levels of governance—from local municipalities to national governments and international bodies— each wielding distinct influences and facing unique challenges in ensuring equitable access to housing. The philosophical and practical commitments to housing as a right necessitate a deep dive into the dynamics of successful and failed policies, and a rigorous exploration of potential reforms aimed at rectifying existing deficiencies and innovating future solutions.

At the local level, governments are often the first line of defense against housing insecurity, tasked with implementing zoning laws, building codes, and housing subsidies that directly affect the availability and affordability of housing. Successful local policies often involve the strategic use of inclusionary zoning, which requires developers to provide a certain percentage of units at below-market rates in new developments. For instance, cities like San Francisco and New York have adopted inclusionary zoning policies that have contributed to an increase in the affordable housing stock by leveraging the private sector's momentum. However, the efficacy of such policies can be hampered by inadequate enforcement and the periodic rollback of regulations due to political pressures, illustrating the delicate balance local authorities must maintain between fostering economic development and securing housing equity.

At the national level, governments have the capacity to enact sweeping reforms through broader legislative frameworks that can standardize protections for renters and homeowners across jurisdictions. Examples of successful national policies include the establishment of robust tenant protections, such as those seen in countries like Germany and Sweden, where long-term rental contracts and strict eviction laws help ensure housing stability for residents. On the other hand, failures are often marked by underfunded public housing programs or poorly conceived mortgage assistance schemes that fail to reach or adequately support their intended beneficiaries. The lessons from these experiences highlight the need for well-funded, well-managed housing initiatives that are responsive to the economic realities of their populations.

Internationally, the role of bodies like the United Nations in promoting housing as a human right is crucial. The UN advocates for global standards and provides frameworks such as the International Covenant on Economic, Social and Cultural Rights, which compels signatory states to work toward the right of everyone to an adequate standard of living, including housing. However, the challenge at the international level often lies in the lack of enforcement mechanisms and the dependency on voluntary compliance by sovereign nations, which can vary widely in their commitment and ability to implement these standards.

The potential for new policies and reforms to more effectively guarantee the right to housing for everyone includes both preventative measures and robust responses to housing crises. Preventative measures could involve the adoption of national rent control standards to prevent exploitative rent increases, or the creation of land banks to develop affordable housing in communities that need it most. In response to housing crises, policies such as rapid-rehousing programs and increased funding for emergency housing services can provide immediate relief to those affected by disasters or economic downturns.

Looking ahead, the future of housing policy must embrace a multifaceted approach that integrates local innovations with national reforms and international cooperation. This approach should be informed by a continuous dialogue between policymakers, housing experts, community activists, and the broader public. Public engagement and activism play pivotal roles in this discourse, serving both to hold governments accountable and to push the boundaries of what can be achieved through collective action.

Furthermore, international cooperation offers a platform for sharing best practices and resources, enhancing the global commitment to housing as a human right. Through forums such as international conferences and treaties, countries can collaborate on addressing global housing challenges, from mass urbanization to the displacement caused by climate change and conflicts.

Securing housing for all as a human right is an ongoing challenge that requires persistent effort, innovative policy-making, and broad-based cooperation. It is a goal that necessitates a deep commitment to justice and equity, demanding that we continuously strive for better, more inclusive policies that uphold the dignity of every individual through the fundamental provision of shelter.

CHAPTER 8
A NEW PATH FOR IMMIGRATION

In an era characterized by unprecedented global mobility, the phenomenon of immigration has emerged as a central fixture in international discourse, presenting a myriad of political, economic, and humanitarian challenges. The movement of people across borders, driven by a confluence of factors including but not limited to war, economic hardship, and climate change, has reached levels that call for a profound reevaluation of how nations manage and respond to immigration. This surge in migratory patterns not only reshapes the demographic landscapes of countries but also tests the ethical frameworks within which national immigration policies are devised and implemented.

The increasing numbers of immigrants and refugees seeking new lives in foreign lands highlight acute crises: from the perilous journeys undertaken by those fleeing conflict zones to the economic migrants attempting to escape poverty, each group seeks something fundamental—a chance at safety, prosperity, and stability. However, the response of host countries to these migrations has varied dramatically, often caught between national security concerns, economic capacities, and international humanitarian obligations, creating a patchwork of policies that reflect diverse priorities and philosophies.

At the heart of this complex tapestry lies the need to address the ethical considerations of immigration policies. The current global landscape, with its stark disparities in how immigrants are received and treated, raises pressing questions about the core values that should guide such policies. It is imperative to ask: What are the responsibilities of states towards those who arrive at their borders? How can policies be structured to uphold the dignity and rights of all individuals, regardless of their nationality or the circumstances that drove them to migrate?

These questions underscore the necessity for immigration reforms grounded in principles of human dignity and justice. Such reforms are not merely administrative necessities but moral imperatives that reflect our collective commitment to uphold the rights inherent to all human beings. The ethical framework for considering immigration policies extends beyond the legal obligations to protect refugees under international law, encompassing a broader spectrum of ethical theories that advocate for fairness, empathy, and the equitable treatment of all individuals.

Philosophers such as Immanuel Kant and John Rawls offer insights that are particularly relevant in this context. Kant's categorical imperative, which commands actions to be undertaken with consideration of their universalizability, prompts a rethinking of policies that might discriminate or unduly harm immigrant populations. Similarly, Rawls's principles of justice, especially the idea that social and economic inequalities should be arranged so that they are to the greatest benefit of the least advantaged, invite policymakers to consider immigration policies that do not marginalize migrants but instead contribute positively to their lives and to the society at large.

The imperative to reform immigration policies to be more ethical and just is not just a philosophical or theoretical exercise but a practical necessity. In societies increasingly characterized by diversity due to global migration, the cohesion, security, and moral integrity of these societies depend significantly on how they treat their most vulnerable members, including immigrants. As such, immigration policy reforms must strive to eliminate discrimination, ensure fairness in the treatment of all individuals, and provide opportunities for immigrants to contribute to their new communities.

The introduction of this chapter sets the stage for a critical examination of the ethical underpinnings of current immigration policies and the compelling need for their reform. It calls for a thoughtful, informed discussion on how nations can navigate the complex interplay of security, economic interests, and humanitarian duties in a way that respects the dignity of all people. The following sections will delve deeper into these ethical considerations, propose specific humane reforms, and explore the roles of various global actors in shaping a just and equitable approach to immigration. This exploration is not only timely but essential in guiding us towards policies that reflect our shared human values and the realities of our interconnected world.

Ethical Foundations of Immigration Policy

The ethical foundations of immigration policy necessitate a principled examination grounded in the universal precepts of human rights, non-discrimination, and the sacrosanct right to asylum. These principles form the cornerstone of a morally coherent approach to immigration, providing a normative framework against which the justice of existing policies can be measured and critiqued.

Universal human rights, as articulated in pivotal documents like the Universal Declaration of Human Rights, assert the intrinsic dignity and the equal and inalienable rights of all members of the human family. This declaration is foundational, offering a global ethos that transcends borders, advocating for rights that are not confined by nationality. Within this framework, immigration policies must be crafted to respect the inherent worth of all individuals, ensuring that immigrants are treated with the same dignity and respect as citizens. Yet, a dissonance often emerges between these universal ideals and the reality of national immigration policies, which frequently prioritize national security and economic interests over the basic rights of migrants.

The principle of non-discrimination, another pillar of ethical immigration policy, mandates that all individuals, regardless of race, nationality, or status, should have equal access to protection and opportunities. This principle challenges policies that might create hierarchies among immigrants, such as those distinguishing between 'high-skilled' and 'low-skilled' workers in ways that devalue certain types of labor and create systemic barriers to integration. It also scrutinizes laws that disproportionately impact migrants from specific regions or backgrounds, highlighting the need for an equitable approach that genuinely reflects the spirit of non-discrimination.

Moreover, the right to asylum holds a special place in immigration ethics, providing refuge to those fleeing persecution and violence. This right, enshrined in international law, is fundamental but frequently under threat by policies that tighten asylum criteria or that implement stringent measures deterring asylum seekers, such as detention at borders or the separation of families. These practices not only contravene the ethical obligation to protect the vulnerable but also erode the moral credibility of states that claim to uphold human rights.

Analyzing how current policies align or conflict with these ethical principles reveals significant gaps. For instance, many nations have faced criticism for their handling of refugee crises, where slow processing of asylum applications and restrictive interpretations of 'persecution' leave many vulnerable individuals in limbo or forcibly return them to harm's way. Similarly, the rise of 'fortress' mentalities in developed countries, prioritizing the fortification of borders over the humanitarian reception of migrants, reflects a troubling shift away from the ethical imperatives of protection and assistance.

Improvements in these areas are urgently needed to realign national policies with ethical standards. This realignment involves not only the removal of discriminatory practices but also the proactive creation of pathways that enhance the dignity and well-being of immigrants. For instance, regularizing the status of undocumented immigrants who contribute to their communities can remove the constant threat of deportation and provide access to essential services, thereby enhancing their ability to participate fully and openly in society.

Additionally, enhancing the transparency and accountability of immigration enforcement agencies is crucial. Oversight mechanisms can ensure that these agencies respect human rights and adhere to non-discriminatory practices in their operations. Moreover, international cooperation is vital in managing global migration flows ethically. Collaborative efforts can lead to shared responsibility for refugees, distribute the benefits and burdens of migration more equitably among countries, and foster global solidarity in the face of humanitarian crises.

The ethical recalibration of immigration policies requires a profound commitment to the principles of human rights, non-discrimination, and the right to asylum. Such a commitment must transcend political and economic considerations, centering ethical imperatives and human dignity in policy-making processes. Only through such a foundational commitment can immigration policies not only meet ethical standards but also contribute to the creation of a more just and humane global society. As we progress, it is imperative that these ethical principles guide not only national responses but also shape the international discourse on migration, ensuring that all people, regardless of their origin or status, are afforded the respect and protection they inherently deserve.

Proposals for Humane Immigration Reforms

To cultivate an immigration policy landscape that is both humane and just, it is imperative to implement reforms grounded in ethical principles and practical efficacy. Such reforms should ensure the dignity of immigrants and refugees while fostering their potential to contribute positively to host societies. Proposals for making pathways to citizenship more accessible, improving conditions within detention centers, and ensuring fair legal processes for asylum seekers and refugees are critical steps toward achieving these goals.

Creating more accessible pathways to citizenship is essential. This approach acknowledges the long-term presence of immigrants in a country and their continuous contributions to its socio-economic fabric. Facilitating a smoother and more equitable route to citizenship can alleviate the insecurities associated with temporary or uncertain immigration statuses and empower immigrants to fully engage in all aspects of societal life. Reducing the complexity and costs of the naturalization process, eliminating prolonged waiting periods, and recognizing the contributions of undocumented immigrants by providing them with a clear and immediate pathway to legal status can significantly enhance the sense of belonging and security among immigrants. This, in turn, contributes to greater social cohesion and economic stability, as naturalized citizens often experience increases in earning potential, consume more goods and services, and contribute more in taxes. Culturally, these citizens enrich the social tapestry of the nation through diverse perspectives and innovations.

Addressing the conditions of immigration detention centers is another vital area for reform. In many detention centers, reports of inadequate healthcare, poor living conditions, and lack of legal representation highlight the urgent need for standards that uphold human rights and dignity. Proposals should include stringent regulations regarding the treatment of detainees, the provision of adequate medical care, access to legal counsel, and the establishment of oversight mechanisms to ensure compliance with these standards. Improving detention center conditions would not only alleviate the immediate suffering of detainees but would also reflect a broader commitment to human rights that can enhance the international standing of the host country. Humanitarian benefits include reduced mental health deterioration among detained individuals, while the potential reduction in the use of detention centers, in favor of community-based processing, can result in significant cost savings and better integration outcomes for immigrants.

Ensuring that asylum seekers and refugees have access to fair legal processes is also essential. This means providing timely and transparent processing of asylum claims, safeguarding the right to appeal, and prohibiting the deportation of individuals to countries where they face imminent danger. Legal reforms should also address the specific vulnerabilities of certain groups, such as unaccompanied minors and victims of trauma, ensuring that their treatment within the asylum process is sensitive and appropriate. For the individuals concerned, access to fair and efficient legal processes can mean the difference between life and death, freedom and persecution. For the host societies, upholding rigorous standards of justice reinforces the rule of law, enhances public confidence in the immigration system, and ensures that the processes are aligned with international human rights obligations.

The broader cultural and economic implications of these immigration reforms are profound. Economically, immigrants who are integrated into society with dignity and respect are more likely to start businesses, create jobs, and innovate in various sectors. Culturally, societies that embrace diversity and provide opportunities for all their members to succeed can expect a richer, more dynamic public life. This environment fosters mutual understanding and respect among all citizens, regardless of their origins.

The proposed immigration reforms aim not only to address the immediate needs of immigrants and refugees but also to enhance the overall well-being of host societies. These reforms, grounded in principles of justice, equity, and human dignity, are essential for building inclusive communities where every individual is valued and where diversity is seen as a strength. The successful implementation of these reforms requires a committed, sustained effort from all sectors of society, underpinned by a shared vision of humanity and justice in our increasingly interconnected world.

Conclusion

We have navigated the complex landscape of immigration policy through a lens that interlaces profound ethical considerations with pragmatic analyses. The urgent need for reform in immigration practices around the world calls for a foundational commitment to the principles of dignity, justice, and equity—tenets that should be enshrined at the heart of all policies affecting the lives of migrants and refugees. These principles are not merely abstract ideals but are essential for the development of humane and effective immigration systems that respect the intrinsic worth of every individual.

We began by establishing the critical importance of addressing immigration from a perspective that respects universal human rights, a principle enshrined in numerous international covenants and declarations. The discussion then transitioned to an examination of the key ethical frameworks that should guide the development of immigration policy. These include the commitment to non-discrimination, the safeguarding of human dignity, and the provision of asylum as a right that transcends national interests. Such frameworks compel us to reconsider how nations can balance sovereign rights with global ethical obligations, especially in contexts that involve vulnerable populations seeking refuge and opportunity.

We also explored specific, actionable reforms aimed at aligning immigration policies more closely with these ethical imperatives. These reforms ranged from creating more accessible pathways to citizenship, which facilitate the integration and full participation of immigrants in host societies, to overhauling detention center conditions to ensure they meet basic standards of human decency. Additionally, the importance of fair legal processes was underscored, emphasizing that justice for immigrants and refugees is a critical component of any democratic society committed to upholding the rule of law.

The potential impact of these proposed reforms is extensive. By implementing policies that are rooted in respect for human rights and social justice, societies can achieve greater social cohesion and stability. Such outcomes not only benefit immigrants but also enrich the cultural, economic, and social fabric of host countries. The integration of immigrants into the workforce, their participation in civic life, and their contributions to cultural diversity can drive innovation and economic growth, proving that inclusive policies are not only morally correct but pragmatically beneficial.

Looking forward, the path to achieving these reforms is not solitary. It requires the concerted effort of global cooperation, where countries work together to share responsibilities and resources in managing migration flows humanely and effectively. International bodies, regional coalitions, and bilateral partnerships must play a pivotal role in crafting coordinated responses to migration challenges. This collaboration is essential in a globalized world where migration impacts are widespread and interconnected.

Moreover, the role of policy advocacy cannot be overstated. Activists, NGOs, and civil society organizations are vital in pushing for changes in immigration law and practice. Their relentless advocacy ensures that the plight of migrants remains visible and that governments are held accountable for their treatment of all individuals within their borders. Public support is equally crucial, as societal attitudes towards immigrants can significantly influence policy directions. Fostering a public ethos that values diversity and human rights can empower political leaders to make courageous decisions in favor of more inclusive and just immigration policies.

The future of immigration policy must be envisioned as a tapestry woven with the threads of dignity, justice, and global cooperation. By adhering to these principles, societies can develop immigration systems that are not only fair and effective but also reflective of a deeper commitment to fostering a world where every individual—regardless of their origin—is treated with respect and offered an equal opportunity to thrive. The journey towards this vision will undoubtedly require resilience, empathy, and an unwavering commitment to the values that underpin our shared humanity.

CHAPTER 9
PUBLIC GOODS AND THE COMMON GOOD

Introduction and The Role of Public Services in Social Justice

Public goods, by their very definition, are commodities or services that are provided without profit to all members of a society, either by the government or a private individual or organization. The quintessential characteristics of public goods, non-excludability and non-rivalry, mean that no one can be effectively excluded from using them, and one person's use does not diminish another's. These features make public goods distinct from private commodities, which can be owned and consumed by individuals and from which others can be excluded.

Within the framework of social justice, public services such as education, healthcare, and transportation become pivotal. These services are not just amenities but essential pillars that support the functioning of equitable societies. They underpin the very notion of the common good—the set of conditions that allows individuals and communities to flourish and achieve well-being. The thesis that public services are foundational for social justice and crucial for fostering equitable communities is rooted in the understanding that access to these services should not be a privilege contingent on wealth or status but a universal right accessible to all.

Education, for instance, serves as a powerful engine of social mobility, offering individuals the tools to improve their economic prospects and engage fully in civic life. The correlation between educational attainment and economic stability is well-documented, with numerous studies demonstrating that higher levels of education lead to higher earnings and lower levels of unemployment. Beyond economic benefits, education enriches individuals' lives through the broadening of perspectives and the fostering of critical thinking skills that are essential for democratic participation.

Similarly, healthcare is another public good that directly impacts the common good by ensuring that all citizens, regardless of their economic status, have access to the services necessary to maintain or improve their health. The non-excludability of this service is critical because health disparities often reflect and exacerbate existing social and economic inequalities. Comprehensive healthcare systems that provide universal coverage not only improve individual well-being but also enhance community health outcomes, thereby reducing public health expenditures and increasing societal productivity.

Transportation also plays a crucial role in social justice by enabling access to other essential services such as jobs, schools, and medical care. Efficient public transportation systems can bridge significant gaps in mobility for underserved populations, facilitating more equitable access to opportunities and resources. The availability of robust public transportation can transform communities by reducing congestion, minimizing emissions, and creating more livable, accessible urban environments.

However, despite the recognized importance of these public goods, access to quality public services is not uniform and often reflects broader societal inequities. Disparities in educational quality across different socio-economic groups, barriers to healthcare access, and inadequate public transportation systems can all perpetuate cycles of disadvantage and inequality. These disparities challenge the integrity of public goods as instruments of the common good and highlight the urgent need for comprehensive strategies to address these inequities.

Addressing these challenges requires a multifaceted approach that includes policy reform, investment in infrastructure, and community engagement. For example, policies that prioritize investment in public schools, particularly in underprivileged areas, can help level the educational playing field. Similarly, healthcare reforms that aim to expand access to medical services regardless of income or background are essential for closing health disparity gaps. In transportation, initiatives that expand and improve public transit can ensure that it serves the needs of all citizens, not just those in densely populated or affluent areas.

The impact of these public services on social mobility, economic equality, and overall quality of life is profound. Data from various case studies across the globe consistently show that when access to quality public services is guaranteed, there are significant improvements in social and economic outcomes. These include better educational achievement, higher employment rates, improved health standards, and more cohesive, sustainable communities.

Reinforcing public services as a pathway to social justice not only enhances individual and community well-being but also strengthens the fabric of society as a whole. By ensuring equitable access to essential services, we uphold the principles of the common good and take concrete steps toward building more just and inclusive communities. This foundational belief in the transformative power of public goods must continue to guide our efforts as we strive to realize the full potential of our collective social enterprise.

Challenges and Barriers in Accessing Quality Public Services

Equitable access to public services, crucial for a functioning society, is impeded by a constellation of structural and systemic barriers that manifest across various sectors. These impediments not only undermine the provision of these essential services but also contribute significantly to the perpetuation of social inequality. Among the most pressing challenges are underfunding, mismanagement, and policies that disproportionately favor private interests over public welfare.

Underfunding is a pervasive issue that severely restricts the quality and reach of public services. This phenomenon is particularly evident in the education sector, where funding gaps between affluent and impoverished districts result in stark disparities in educational quality and outcomes. In many jurisdictions, public schools rely heavily on local property taxes for funding. This system inherently disadvantages those in economically depressed areas, perpetuating a cycle of inequality as these schools are unable to provide the same quality of education, facilities, and resources that schools in wealthier areas can. The ramifications are profound, affecting student performance, graduation rates, and subsequent access to higher education and employment opportunities. Thus, the underfunding of public schools not only compromises educational attainment but also reinforces socioeconomic barriers.

In the healthcare sector, mismanagement and inefficiency often lead to suboptimal care delivery and resource utilization. This mismanagement can take various forms, from bureaucratic inefficiencies that delay the provision of care to poor allocation of resources that fails to meet community health needs. For instance, in some public healthcare systems, there are significant delays in treatment due to overwhelmed facilities and insufficient staffing, which can exacerbate health issues and lead to poor health outcomes. Moreover, mismanagement can also manifest in the inadequate response to public health crises, where a lack of coordination and preparedness can result in severe consequences for the most vulnerable populations. Such systemic failures not only erode trust in public healthcare systems but also widen health disparities, as those with means may turn to private care options that are often inaccessible to lower-income individuals.

Furthermore, policies that favor private interests can also restrict access to quality public services. In the realm of public safety, for instance, the privatization of certain services can lead to unequal levels of protection and response. Private security companies may provide enhanced services in wealthier areas, leaving economically disadvantaged communities with inferior public safety services. This not only fosters a sense of insecurity but also perpetuates a two-tier system of public safety that prioritizes wealthier citizens. Additionally, the increasing privatization of utilities such as water and electricity can lead to higher costs and reduced access for poorer households, exacerbating the challenges faced by these communities.

The intersection of these barriers significantly contributes to social inequality by creating and reinforcing divisions along socioeconomic lines. Individuals and communities deprived of quality public education face limited economic opportunities, those with inadequate healthcare remain in poorer health and have shorter life expectancies, and regions with insufficient public safety measures are prone to higher rates of crime and violence. Each of these factors plays a role in a vicious cycle of poverty and disenfranchisement, stifling social mobility and entrenching systemic inequities.

Addressing these barriers requires a comprehensive approach that not only increases funding for under-resourced public services but also improves management practices to ensure efficiency and accountability. Moreover, it necessitates a shift in policymaking to prioritize public over private interests, ensuring that public services remain accessible to all, regardless of socioeconomic status. Only through such multifaceted efforts can societies begin to dismantle the structural impediments to social equality, paving the way for a more just and equitable distribution of public goods. This endeavor, while complex, is essential for the realization of a society in which every individual has access to the services necessary for their well-being and success.

Strategies for Enhancing Public Goods Provision

Addressing the deficiencies in the provision of public goods requires a strategic approach that encompasses both structural reforms and innovative strategies to expand access and enhance the quality of public services. Effective solutions involve a combination of increased public funding, improved management practices, and legislative reforms, alongside novel approaches like public-private partnerships and community-based management. These initiatives are designed not merely to patch existing gaps but to overhaul systems in ways that sustain long-term improvements and equitable access.

A foundational strategy is to increase public funding for critical services such as education, healthcare, and transportation. Adequate funding is essential for maintaining infrastructure, hiring qualified professionals, and ensuring that services meet the needs of all citizens, particularly those in underserved areas. For instance, in the educational sector, increased investment could support the reduction of class sizes, provision of modern learning materials, and maintenance of school facilities, which are crucial for improving student outcomes. In healthcare, greater funding can enhance the availability of medical services, reduce wait times, and increase the accessibility of preventative care, thus improving overall public health outcomes.

Beyond funding, the reform of management practices in public service provision is imperative. This includes adopting transparency and accountability measures that ensure resources are used efficiently and effectively. Implementing modern management information systems can help track service delivery and resource use, identify inefficiencies, and promote data-driven decision-making. For example, in public healthcare systems, robust health information systems can manage patient data across different facilities, ensuring consistent and coordinated care that improves patient outcomes and optimizes resource allocation.

Legislative reforms also play a crucial role in ensuring that public services are prioritized and protected. Laws and regulations can be designed to safeguard funding, prevent the privatization of essential services, and ensure that all citizens have equitable access to these services. Legislation can also support the maintenance and expansion of public goods, creating legal frameworks that facilitate rather than hinder the provision of essential services to the population.

In addition to traditional approaches, the potential for innovative strategies such as public-private partnerships (PPPs) and community-based management should be explored to enhance the efficiency and effectiveness of public service delivery. PPPs involve collaboration between government entities and private companies to fund, construct, and manage public services. This model can bring in private sector efficiencies and capital to public projects, speeding up completion times and bringing in advanced expertise while keeping the public interests at the forefront. For instance, in the development of public transportation infrastructure, such partnerships can enable the rapid construction and better maintenance of facilities without compromising service quality or accessibility.

Community-based management of public services offers another innovative approach, particularly effective in sectors like water supply and primary healthcare. By involving local communities in the management of services, this approach ensures that the services are tailored to the unique needs of the community, enhancing relevance and effectiveness. Moreover, community involvement increases transparency and accountability, as local stakeholders have a direct interest in the optimal functioning of these services.

The synthesis of these strategies—enhanced funding, management reforms, legislative action, and innovative collaboration models—presents a robust blueprint for transforming the provision of public goods. The potential impact of these strategies extends beyond immediate improvements in service delivery to broader socio-economic benefits, including enhanced social mobility, economic stability, and overall quality of life.

The strategic enhancement of public goods provision through a combination of traditional reforms and innovative approaches can significantly improve the quality and accessibility of essential services. By ensuring that public services are both efficient and equitable, we can better meet the needs of all citizens and move closer to realizing the common good in a tangible and meaningful way. This comprehensive approach is not only a response to the challenges faced but also an anticipatory move towards future-proofing our public services against upcoming demographic, economic, and environmental challenges.

Conclusion

In synthesizing the discussions of this chapter, it becomes evident that public goods are not merely functional amenities but are pivotal in cementing the foundation for social justice and the common good. As explored, the intrinsic characteristics of public goods—non-excludability and non-rivalry—ensure that these resources should ideally serve not just a few, but all members of a community, thereby promoting a fair and equitable society. The commitment to maintaining and enhancing public goods such as education, healthcare, and transportation is thus a commitment to enhancing the quality of life for every citizen, regardless of their socio-economic status.

The role of public goods in advancing social justice is profound. Access to quality education opens the doors to opportunity and social mobility, while equitable healthcare services ensure that all individuals can lead healthy, productive lives. Efficient public transportation systems enable access to jobs, educational opportunities, and healthcare services, thereby knitting together the diverse threads of a community into a cohesive whole. These services are the bedrock upon which societies can build a more just and equitable existence for all their members.

However, the chapter also illuminated the various challenges and barriers that prevent equitable access to these vital services. Underfunding, mismanagement, and policies skewed towards private interests rather than public welfare are significant hurdles. These challenges not only degrade the quality of public services but also deepen existing social inequalities, thus detracting from the common good. Addressing these barriers requires diligent, ongoing efforts and a reorientation of policies to refocus on the public interest.

The necessity for reform is clear, and the strategies for enhancing the provision of public goods are manifold. Increased funding, improved management practices, legislative reforms, and innovative approaches such as public-private partnerships and community-based management all hold the potential to significantly improve public services. Each strategy offers unique benefits and can be adapted to local contexts to meet specific community needs. However, the successful implementation of these reforms is contingent upon the active involvement and collaboration of various stakeholders, including government officials, policymakers, community leaders, and citizens.

As we conclude, it is crucial to underscore the urgent need for collective action. Policymakers must prioritize the expansion and enhancement of public goods, ensuring that policies are not only designed with the public's best interests at heart but are also resilient against encroachment by private interests. Community leaders can serve as vital advocates for change, galvanizing local support for reforms and ensuring that the voices of the most affected are heard in policy-making processes. Citizens, too, have a role to play. Through informed voting, community involvement, and advocacy, individuals can help shape the policies that affect their lives and ensure that public services truly contribute to the common good.

This chapter calls for a renewed commitment to public goods as a cornerstone of social justice and the common good. By advocating for and implementing strategic reforms, we can ensure that public services not only meet the needs of today's populations but are also equitable and sustainable for generations to come. Let this be a call to action for all stakeholders to engage deeply with the principles outlined and work tirelessly towards a society where public goods enhance the well-being of every community member. The path forward is challenging but essential; let us advance with the resolve that our collective efforts will forge a more just, equitable, and flourishing society.

CHAPTER 10
PHILOSOPHY AGAINST WAR

*Introduction and Philosophical
Critiques of Militarism*

Militarism, characterized by the glorification of military prowess and an aggressive preparedness for war, permeates not only political doctrines but also seeps into the cultural fabric of societies, often shaping national identity and public policy. Historically, militarism has been both a precipitant and a consequence of conflict, fostering an environment where power is predominantly measured in terms of military capability. The cultural implications are profound, as they embed a warrior ethos in the collective consciousness, often at the expense of peace and humanitarian values.

The philosophical critique of militarism challenges this paradigm, advocating for a reevaluation of ethical priorities towards peace and

213

international solidarity. Philosophy, in this context, serves as a rigorous lens through which the assumptions underpinning militaristic policies are examined and contested. This critique draws strength from a rich tradition of thought, from Immanuel Kant's perpetual peace to Leo Tolstoy's impassioned advocacy for nonviolence, and extends to contemporary philosophers who interrogate the moral justifications of modern warfare.

Kant, in his seminal essay "Perpetual Peace," argues that the civil constitution of every state should be republican, as this form of governance entails a separation of the executive and legislative powers, a condition he deemed necessary for a peaceable federation of states. According to Kant, such a federation, grounded in the principles of freedom, equality, and independence, precludes the inclination towards militarism by aligning the citizens' interests with peaceful coexistence. Kant's philosophy introduces the concept of cosmopolitan right, which insists on the hospitality and non-hostility towards foreigners, thus laying one of the earliest foundations for internationalism opposed to militaristic expansion.

Contrastingly, Tolstoy takes a more radical stance, denouncing all forms of violence and militarism through his Christian anarchist perspective. In his works like "War and Peace" and "The Kingdom of God Is Within You," Tolstoy espouses the belief that true Christian ethics contradict the state's advocacy for militarism and war. He argues that the Christian call to turn the other cheek is incompatible with the state's call to arms, thereby presenting a moral dilemma to any adherent of the faith. Tolstoy's critique extends to the societal norms that glorify war, challenging the populace to recognize the inherent contradiction between the teachings of peace and the practices of war.

In the contemporary philosophical arena, debates around just war theory and realism further enrich the discourse on militarism. Just war theory, which attempts to provide a framework for justifying when and how war might be permissible, grapples with ethical dilemmas such as proportionality, legitimate authority, and last resort. While just war theory offers a more measured approach to militarism, it is not without its critics, who argue that it too easily lends moral sanction to war, often underestimating the long-term impacts on societies and the environment.

Realism, on the other hand, offers a starkly different view by prioritizing national interest and security over ethical considerations, essentially accepting war and conflict as inevitable aspects of international relations. Realist arguments often support militarism by advocating that a strong military capability is essential for survival in an anarchic international system. This perspective, however, is challenged by the ethical imperatives that call for international cooperation and peacebuilding as more sustainable and morally sound approaches to securing global peace.

The philosophical inquiry into militarism thus serves not only to critique the existing militaristic policies but also to advocate for a paradigm shift towards policies that prioritize human dignity and international solidarity. By engaging with these varied philosophical arguments, we gain a deeper understanding of the complex ethical landscapes that inform decisions about war and peace. This understanding is crucial for developing strategies that seek not only to mitigate the harms associated with militarism but also to foster a global community committed to lasting peace and cooperative international relations.

DAYTON

The Ethical Imperative of Peace

The ethical imperative of peace is underpinned by a profound commitment to human rights, justice, and global empathy, forming a moral framework that both condemns the destructiveness of war and promotes the preservation of human dignity. This framework is not merely aspirational but rooted in rigorous philosophical traditions that articulate the necessity of peace as a foundational element of a just society. Within this discourse, the philosophies of non-violence advocated by figures such as Mahatma Gandhi and Martin Luther King Jr. play a pivotal role, offering both a moral critique of violence and a practical methodology for social and political change.

The call for peace emerges from an understanding that war invariably leads to suffering and degradation of human life, violating the basic human rights to safety, security, and integrity.

Philosophical arguments supporting peace often invoke the concept of justice, particularly distributive justice, which seeks to ensure that all individuals have access to the resources necessary to lead fulfilling lives. From this perspective, war disrupts not only the immediate welfare of individuals but also the broader social structures that support justice and equitable distribution of resources. The destruction and resource drain caused by armed conflicts hinder developmental efforts, deepen inequality, and perpetuate cycles of violence, making peace a prerequisite for any meaningful progress toward global justice.

Global empathy extends these considerations by fostering a sense of shared humanity and mutual responsibility among people across different nations and cultures. This empathetic connection discourages the dehumanization often associated with militaristic rhetoric and promotes understanding and cooperation between diverse groups. The ethos of empathy challenges the insular narratives that often justify aggression and highlights the interconnectedness of all human beings, asserting that the well-being of others is intrinsically linked to our own.

The philosophical stances of Mahatma Gandhi and Martin Luther King Jr. significantly enrich the discourse on non-violence and its role in achieving peace. Gandhi's philosophy of Satyagraha, or 'truth-force,' proposed that true power derives from adherence to truth and non-violence. He believed that non-violent resistance, rooted in moral strength, could effectively oppose and transform unjust systems. Gandhi's methods of civil disobedience influenced numerous movements worldwide, demonstrating that non-violent approaches could achieve profound social and political changes without resorting to violence.

Similarly, Martin Luther King Jr. adapted Gandhian principles to the context of the American Civil Rights Movement, advocating for non-violence as both an ethical doctrine and a practical tactic for combating racial segregation and injustice. King argued that non-violence was not a passive submission to evil but a powerful way to resist oppression without undermining the humanity of the oppressor. By doing so, non-violence seeks to win over opponents and foster reconciliation, thereby laying the groundwork for a more peaceful and just society.

The relevance of these philosophies in contemporary discussions on peace and conflict resolution cannot be overstated. In an era where conflicts frequently arise from deep-seated racial, religious, and cultural divisions, the teachings of Gandhi and King offer viable strategies for bridging divides and addressing grievances through empathy and dialogue rather than force. Their emphasis on moral courage and the transformative power of non-violence provides critical insights for contemporary peace movements and for policymakers striving to resolve conflicts without escalation.

The ethical imperative of peace, grounded in human rights, justice, and global empathy, and illuminated by the philosophies of non-violence, presents a compelling framework for addressing the root causes of conflict. It advocates for a world where disputes are resolved through dialogue and mutual understanding, where the structures that support peace are strengthened rather than undermined by aggression, and where societies are built on the principles of equity and compassion. This vision for peace is not only a moral obligation but a practical necessity, urging us to rethink our approaches to conflict and to work tirelessly towards a more harmonious and sustainable global community.

Pathways to Peace and International Solidarity

In addressing the challenges of achieving global peace and fostering international solidarity, it is crucial to delineate practical pathways that not only mitigate the conditions leading to conflict but actively promote harmonious international relations. Such pathways involve comprehensive strategies including disarmament, the enhancement of conflict resolution mechanisms, and the fortification of international law and cooperation. The efficacy of these strategies often hinges on the robust engagement of international organizations, treaties, and a spectrum of both governmental and non-governmental agencies.

Disarmament stands as a fundamental strategy in the quest for peace. It entails the reduction or elimination of certain classes of weapons, particularly nuclear arsenals and other weapons of mass destruction, which pose the greatest threat to global security. The rationale for disarmament is rooted in the recognition that the mere existence of these weapons perpetuates a culture of fear and mistrust that can escalate into armed conflict. Initiatives such as the Treaty on the Non-Proliferation of Nuclear Weapons (NPT) and the recent Treaty on the Prohibition of Nuclear Weapons (TPNW) exemplify international efforts to not only prevent the spread of nuclear weapons but also to promote their complete elimination. However, the success of disarmament policies requires universal cooperation and compliance, which can only be achieved through enhanced diplomatic engagement and the strengthening of verification mechanisms that ensure transparency and trust among nations.

Beyond disarmament, the development of effective conflict resolution mechanisms is essential. Such mechanisms include diplomacy, mediation, and peacekeeping operations, which are designed to address and resolve conflicts without recourse to violence. The United Nations plays a pivotal role in this regard, offering a forum for negotiation and dispute resolution through its various agencies, including the Security Council and the General Assembly. Moreover, specialized bodies such as the International Court of Justice and the International Criminal Court contribute to upholding international law and adjudicating disputes that could otherwise lead to conflict. These institutions, by providing legal and peaceful means to resolve international disputes, reinforce the rule of law and help to stabilize tense situations that could potentially escalate into broader conflicts.

Strengthening international law and cooperation involves the continual development and enforcement of international treaties that govern state behavior. Treaties such as the Geneva Conventions, which set the standards for international law regarding humanitarian concerns during war, play a crucial role in limiting the barbarity of conflict and providing protection for those who are most vulnerable. Furthermore, international cooperation is enhanced through regional organizations such as the European Union, the African Union, and ASEAN, which facilitate political and economic collaboration between member states and help to mediate tensions within these regions.

The roles played by various international organizations, governmental agencies, and non-governmental organizations (NGOs) are critical in advocating for and maintaining peace. NGOs, in particular, play a unique role by raising awareness, mobilizing public opinion, and often providing direct mediation and conflict resolution services in areas affected by war. Organizations such as Amnesty International, Human Rights Watch, and the International Red Cross and Red

Crescent Movement not only provide humanitarian assistance but also work tirelessly to hold violators of international law accountable, thereby contributing to the broader efforts of peacebuilding.

The pathways to achieving peace and fostering international solidarity are complex and multifaceted. They require the concerted efforts of the international community, including states, international organizations, and civil society, to embrace a multi-pronged approach that includes disarmament, the strengthening of conflict resolution mechanisms, and the robust enforcement of international law. By committing to these strategies, the global community can move closer to a world where peace is not merely a distant ideal, but a tangible reality, and where international relations are governed not by the dynamics of power and fear but by the principles of justice and mutual respect. This pursuit of peace demands not only political will and diplomatic effort but also a foundational commitment to the values that underpin a just and equitable international order.

Conclusion

We have traversed the profound philosophical landscape that critiques militarism, advocating a paradigm shift towards peace and international solidarity. This discourse has explored the intrinsic values and ethical imperatives that should guide our approach to international relations and conflict resolution. As we conclude, it is essential to reinforce these philosophical underpinnings and the critical necessity of fostering a global environment where peace is not merely aspirational but a fundamental objective of all societal and international actions.

The philosophical stance against militarism is grounded in a deep-seated commitment to human dignity and the sanctity of life. Militarism, with its inherent glorification of war and military might, often undermines these values, promoting a culture where conflicts are resolved through force rather than dialogue and mutual understanding. The critiques presented by eminent thinkers like Immanuel Kant, Leo Tolstoy, and their contemporary counterparts have illuminated the moral failures of militarism and the subsequent human suffering it entails. These philosophical perspectives argue compellingly for a world where peace is maintained not by the threat of destruction but through the bonds of shared humanity and reciprocal respect among nations.

Moreover, the discussion has highlighted the vital need for sustained peace and international solidarity. In an interconnected world, the ripple effects of conflict are no longer confined to specific regions but can impact global stability and security. The ethical imperative for peace extends beyond the cessation of armed conflict to the creation of systems and structures that prevent the onset of war. This involves addressing the root causes of conflict, such as poverty, inequality, and political oppression, which are often exacerbated by militaristic policies. The promotion of international solidarity—through cooperative global governance, adherence to international law, and a commitment to multilateralism—is essential in this context, as it fosters a collective approach to solving global issues that could otherwise lead to conflict.

The path forward requires a concerted effort from global leaders, policymakers, and citizens to embrace and operationalize the principles of peace and non-violence. It is a call to action for those in positions of power to rethink security not as a function of military strength but as a product of cooperative peacebuilding efforts. Policymakers must craft laws and frameworks that prioritize peace and human rights, actively dismantling the infrastructure of militarism that perpetuates cycles of violence. International organizations and treaties must be supported and strengthened to enforce these norms and hold states accountable to their commitments.

Citizens, too, play a crucial role in advocating for peace. Through education, activism, and civic engagement, individuals can help shape public policies and create a culture that values peace and rejects war as a means of resolving disputes. The power of the populace in democratic societies, in particular, must be leveraged to demand that elected officials adhere to principles of peace and justice in their governance and foreign policy.

In essence, the pursuit of a peaceful future is both a moral imperative and a practical necessity for the survival and flourishing of humanity. It requires a shift in values and priorities from all sectors of society and a renewed commitment to the principles that uphold our common humanity. As we continue to face new global challenges, the lessons distilled from the philosophical critiques of militarism must guide our collective journey towards a world where peace, justice, and solidarity reign supreme. This journey, while undoubtedly fraught with challenges, is the only path that leads to a sustainable future for all.

CHAPTER 11

INTEGRATING PERSONAL AND PROFESSIONAL INSIGHTS FOR A BROADER VISION

Reflecting on the Journey

As we draw near the conclusion of this exploration, it is pertinent to reflect upon the journey we have undertaken together through the pages of this book. From philosophical musings on war and peace to critical examinations of public policy and societal structures, the themes we have encountered are both diverse and deeply interconnected. Each discussion, enriched by a spectrum of theoretical insights and practical analyses, has not only sought to challenge prevailing norms but also to propose pathways towards a more just and equitable society.

My own journey, both in the professional realms of government and through the profoundly personal experiences as a cancer patient, has provided a unique vantage point from which to view these issues. These experiences have not merely influenced my perspective; they have deeply informed and shaped the conclusions drawn throughout this discourse. Serving as a government official offered me firsthand insights into the machinations of policymaking, the intricate balancing acts of governance, and the often-stark disparity between policy intent and its implementation. This vantage has provided a practical framework for understanding how policies can be structured to better serve the public and how they might be reimagined to foster broader societal well-being.

Simultaneously, my battle with cancer introduced me to the vulnerabilities that come with being a patient in a sprawling healthcare system. This experience exposed me to the stark realities of the healthcare landscape, including the gaps in care and the variability in patient experience based on socioeconomic status. It heightened my awareness of the critical need for policies that not only address healthcare accessibility and affordability but also emphasize the quality of care and the dignity of patients. This personal health crisis thus became a lens through which I viewed not only healthcare policy but all forms of public service, underscoring the profound impact of these systems on individual lives.

Together, these professional and personal experiences have served as a dual lens through which the themes discussed in this book have been filtered. They exemplify broader societal issues—the imperfections of well-intended policies, the gaps between policy and practice, and the often-overlooked human elements within these systems. My experiences have reinforced the necessity of designing policies that are not only effective in their economic or administrative goals but are also compassionate and responsive to the human conditions they aim to improve.

As we consider these reflections, we set the stage for a deeper discussion on how these individual experiences connect to larger societal challenges and potential solutions. Each theme addressed in the preceding chapters—from the ethics of war to the provision of public goods—can be seen through this personal-professional prism, enriching our understanding and adding complexity to our discussions. This approach does not merely add a subjective element to the discourse but enhances it, providing real-world stakes and implications to the theoretical frameworks and proposed reforms.

In contemplating the integration of these diverse themes through the unique perspectives provided by my experiences, we are reminded of the complexity of societal issues and the multifaceted approaches required to address them. The following sections will delve deeper into how these personal insights not only illuminate specific challenges but also suggest holistic and integrative solutions that can lead to substantial societal improvements. This reflection is not an end in itself but a precursor to a more profound call to action, urging us to reimagine and reform the structures within which we operate for a future that upholds the dignity and welfare of every individual.

Lessons from Government Service: Policy, People, and Impact

Navigating the corridors of government as a public official provided a profound insight into the complexities of policymaking, the intricate dynamics of bureaucratic structures, and the palpable impact of administrative decisions on the citizenry. My tenure was marked by direct involvement in several initiatives aimed at enhancing public welfare and improving the mechanisms through which services were delivered. These experiences not only enriched my understanding of the governance process but also illuminated the multifarious challenges and opportunities inherent in public service.

One pivotal area of involvement was the reform of healthcare policies, particularly aimed at increasing accessibility and affordability for marginalized populations. The policy aimed to streamline healthcare delivery and expand coverage, addressing disparities that often left the most vulnerable without necessary care. The challenges in implementing these changes were manifold, including resistance from established interests within the healthcare industry, the logistical hurdles of overhauling longstanding procedures, and the political negotiations required to garner sufficient support.

The process of pushing these healthcare reforms taught me the critical importance of coalition-building and the need for clear, communicative leadership. It highlighted how policy reforms could stall or be derailed by entrenched practices and the importance of persistent advocacy and informed strategy. Yet, the successes of these reforms—marked by increased patient satisfaction, broader coverage, and improved health outcomes—demonstrated the profound impact that thoughtful, well-implemented policies can have. They served as a testament to the potential for government action to effect meaningful change and significantly enhance the quality of life for individuals.

Another significant area of focus during my government service was the reform of public administration systems to increase transparency and efficiency. The initiative aimed to reduce bureaucratic red tape that often-hampered public service delivery and to implement new technologies that could facilitate more streamlined processes. This endeavor faced its own set of challenges, particularly the inertia of traditional systems and the skepticism of public officials accustomed to established routines. Overcoming these barriers required a combination of technological innovation, training programs, and a cultural shift towards valuing efficiency and accountability.

The successes in this sector were particularly rewarding. The introduction of digital platforms for service delivery, for instance, not only improved efficiency but also made governmental processes more accessible to the public. This digital transformation allowed citizens to engage with services more directly and conveniently, reducing frustration and increasing trust in government processes. The positive feedback from the public and the measurable improvements in service delivery times were clear indicators of the initiative's impact.

Reflecting on these experiences underscores the multifaceted nature of governance and the myriad factors that influence policy outcomes. It also reinforces the necessity for ongoing reform across various sectors. Each success and setback have provided valuable lessons on the complexities of implementing change within public systems. These insights have been integral to shaping a broader understanding of effective governance and its potential to drive substantial societal progress.

As a former government official and now government bureaucrat deeply invested in the welfare of my community, these reflections not only inform my critique of existing systems but also fuel my advocacy for thoughtful, inclusive, and responsive governance. The potential for positive societal impact through well-crafted policy is immense, but realizing it requires perseverance, innovation, and a commitment to the public good that must persist beyond individual tenures and administrative cycles. This understanding is crucial as we consider the pathways forward, not just in government but in all institutions tasked with serving the public interest.

Insights from Personal Health Battles: Resilience and Reform

My personal battle with terminal Stage IV colon cancer has been one of profound physical, emotional, and intellectual upheaval. Navigating this deeply personal journey has not only transformed my perspective on healthcare systems but has also underscored the critical importance of patient rights, healthcare policy, and the need for comprehensive and compassionate public services. This experience has forged a unique lens through which I perceive the intricate interplay between individual vulnerability, resilience, and systemic reform.

Diagnosed with terminal Stage IV colon cancer, I was immediately thrust into the labyrinthine structure of the healthcare system. The complexities of insurance policies, treatment protocols, and the logistical challenges of scheduling appointments became my new reality. The immense emotional toll of confronting one's mortality was compounded by the administrative and bureaucratic hurdles that patients often face. This journey from diagnosis to ongoing treatment illuminated the deep fissures within our healthcare system—fissures that not only complicate access to care but also exacerbate the emotional and physical suffering of patients.

One of the most poignant insights from this experience is the vulnerability inherent in being a patient. Despite a lifetime of professional accomplishments and a deep understanding of healthcare policy, I found myself overwhelmed and disoriented by the gravity of the diagnosis and the intricacies of treatment. The initial shock of diagnosis was followed by a grueling regimen of surgeries, chemotherapy, immunotherapy, and radiation that tested the limits of my physical and mental endurance. Throughout this period, it became evident how critical it is for healthcare systems to be patient-centered and responsive to the multifaceted needs of those battling life-threatening illnesses.

The emotional and physical challenges I faced have been harrowing. The side effects of chemotherapy—nausea, fatigue, neuropathy—often left me debilitated, while the uncertainty of my prognosis weighed heavily on my psyche. In these moments, the support of empathetic healthcare providers, the compassion of family and friends, and the clarity of accessible information became lifelines that sustained me. These experiences have galvanized my advocacy for better healthcare services and patient care standards. They highlighted the importance of not just treating the disease but also addressing the holistic needs of patients through supportive care, counseling, and transparent communication.

From a policy perspective, my battle with cancer has revealed the dire need for reforms that ensure healthcare systems are equitable, compassionate, and comprehensive. The variability in care quality based on socioeconomic status, geographic location, and insurance coverage is deeply troubling. My privileged position as a government worker and an educated individual afforded me access to quality care, yet many others are not as fortunate. The disparities in healthcare access and outcomes are unacceptable, and this has fueled my commitment to advocating for policies that prioritize universal coverage, patient rights, and quality standards.

Vulnerability, often perceived as weakness, is an intrinsic aspect of the human condition, particularly when facing terminal illness. Yet, within this vulnerability lies immense strength—the resilience to endure, to hope, and to strive for a meaningful life despite the circumstances. This interplay between vulnerability and resilience is not just personal but systemic. It reflects the need for healthcare systems to recognize and address the inherent vulnerabilities of patients while empowering them to navigate their journeys with dignity and agency.

Connecting these personal experiences back to the themes of public service and societal reform, it is evident that our healthcare systems must evolve to meet the challenges of a diverse and aging population. The need for compassionate, comprehensive care extends beyond the walls of hospitals and clinics to encompass broader social support systems. Public services must be designed to recognize the holistic needs of individuals, particularly those facing critical health challenges, and to ensure that no one is left behind due to systemic inefficiencies or inequities.

My journey as a cancer patient has not only reshaped my understanding of healthcare systems but has also reinforced the importance of patient-centered policies and the profound need for resilience in the face of adversity. It has reaffirmed my belief in the power of compassionate public services to transform lives and has inspired a renewed commitment to advocating for a society where vulnerability is met with empathy, and where every individual receives the care and support, they deserve.

Synthesizing Professional and Personal Insights

In synthesizing my personal and professional experiences, I have gained an intricate perspective that has fundamentally enriched my understanding of public policy and its implementation. The dual lens of my tenure in government coupled with my deeply personal journey through a severe health crisis has provided a profound appreciation for the nuanced interplay between the structural mechanisms of policy and the human narratives they impact. This synthesis underscores the imperative for a holistic approach to policymaking that prioritizes not only systemic efficiency but also the empathy required to meet human needs effectively.

During my career as a government official, I engaged directly with the multifaceted nature of policy formulation and execution, which afforded me insights into the intricate challenges of implementing sustainable changes within established bureaucratic frameworks. These professional experiences highlighted the potential of governance to effectuate significant social advancements and mitigate disparities.

However, they also revealed the complexities inherent in modifying entrenched systems, where policy initiatives must navigate through layers of political inertia and competing interests.

Contrastingly, my confrontation with terminal Stage IV colon cancer exposed me to the vulnerabilities inherent in being a recipient of healthcare policies, which I had once helped to craft. This ordeal illuminated the frequent disconnect between the theoretical efficiencies of healthcare policies and the realities of their execution on the ground. Navigating the healthcare system from the patient's viewpoint revealed gaps in care delivery and inconsistencies that often exacerbate the suffering of those they aim to serve. The personal battles with the healthcare apparatus underscored the profound impact of these policies on individual lives, highlighting an urgent need for reforms that transcend mere operational efficiency to embrace a more compassionate approach to healthcare delivery.

The intersection of these diverse yet interconnected experiences has clarified the necessity for policies that are conceived and implemented with an acute awareness of their broadest impacts. This approach requires an amalgamation of rigorous policy frameworks with a deep sensitivity to the human conditions they affect—a paradigm where efficiency and empathy are not mutually exclusive but are interdependent and reinforcing.

Such an enlightened approach to policymaking advocates for the development of policies that not only fulfill administrative metrics but also respond dynamically to the human elements at their core. For instance, in the realm of healthcare, this perspective champions a patient-centric model that integrates medical excellence with holistic support systems addressing mental, emotional, and social health. It calls for a redefinition of healthcare quality that encompasses patient dignity, access to information, and support for the psychological aspects of medical treatment.

Furthermore, in the broader canvas of public administration, adopting a holistic policy approach necessitates the redesign of service delivery to prioritize user experience and accessibility. It involves a shift towards human-centered design principles in public services, which advocate for seamless, transparent, and responsive interactions between the citizenry and the state. This model promotes an integration of services that recognizes the interconnected needs of individuals, advocating for policies that are crafted not from the top down but from the center outwards, keeping the citizen at the core of policy innovation.

In advocating for a policy landscape that is both effective and humane, there is a call to action for policymakers, administrators, and civic leaders to foster environments where policies are not merely enacted but are lived and experienced positively by the populace. This call supports a governance ethos that values empathy as much as it does efficiency, urging a recommitment to public service as a noble pursuit aimed at enhancing the welfare and dignity of the community.

Thus, the synthesis of professional insights and personal experiences not only enriches the discourse on public policy but also implores a more compassionate and comprehensive approach to governance. It is a call for a paradigmatic shift towards policies that recognize and respect the complexity of human needs, advocating for a future where public services elevate the quality of life for all members of society in profound and meaningful ways.

POLICIES & PAIN

A Call to Action

As we draw the threads of this discourse to a close, it is incumbent upon us to reflect on the overarching themes that have permeated the fabric of this book. The journey through the various philosophical and practical landscapes has been guided by a dual lens of personal experience and professional insight, each illuminating the other, thereby enriching our understanding of the complex interplay between individual narratives and systemic structures. This synthesis has reinforced the imperative for comprehensive reforms in public policy and service delivery, informed by a profound commitment to justice, equity, and efficacy.

The discussions presented have underscored the critical need for a paradigm shift in how policies are conceived and implemented. Drawing from the philosophical critiques of militarism, the advocacy for public goods, and the integration of personal health challenges, we have navigated through the necessity for policies that are not only efficient but are also imbued with empathy and respect for human dignity. These are not merely theoretical ideals but are foundational principles that should drive the formulation and execution of public policies.

Throughout the book, we have advocated for a holistic approach to governance that considers both the systemic and human elements inherent in policymaking. This approach necessitates a departure from traditional bureaucratic processes to embrace a more human-centered design in public services. Such a shift is vital not only in healthcare, where the stakes are profoundly personal, but across all domains of public administration where the impact of policies reverberates through the lives of citizens.

In summoning the collective will for reform, we issue a call to action to policymakers, practitioners, and citizens. It is a call for vigorous engagement with the processes that shape our social, political, and economic realities. Policymakers are urged to craft laws and regulations that reflect an acute sensitivity to the human conditions they affect, striving for systems that are transparent, accountable, and inclusive. Practitioners across all sectors are called upon to advocate for and implement practices that prioritize individual well-being as the cornerstone of professional efficacy. Citizens, too, are encouraged to participate actively in the democratic processes, to hold their leaders accountable, and to demand systems that serve the public good with integrity and compassion.

As we look toward the future, there is an enduring hope and a steadfast belief in the power of informed advocacy and compassionate governance to effectuate meaningful change. This hope is not naively optimistic but is based on the tangible successes witnessed when empathy and equity guide public endeavors. It is a hope that is fortified by the resilience observed in communities that rally for justice and the relentless spirit of individuals who advocate for change against daunting odds.

Reflecting personally on this journey, my experiences both as a cancer patient navigating the challenges of healthcare systems and as a government official grappling with the intricacies of policymaking have profoundly shaped my perspective on the power and potential of public service. These experiences have imbued me with an unshakeable conviction in the necessity for policies that genuinely serve and uplift the populace. They have taught me that meaningful change is indeed possible when driven by a deep-seated commitment to the principles of justice, empathy, and collective well-being.

Thus, as we conclude this exploration, let us carry forward the lessons learned with a renewed commitment to transforming our systems. Let us continue to strive for a world where governance is not just a mechanism of power but a tool for real human upliftment, where every policy and every practice is imbued with the dignity and respect that each individual deserves. Together, informed by our shared experiences and guided by our collective conscience, we can forge a path toward a more just, equitable, and compassionate world.

About the Author

Dr. Dayton is a distinguished public policy expert with extensive experience in government, veterans' affairs, and public health. Raised in California's Central Valley in a middle-class, union household, he was instilled with the values of education and advocacy from a young age. Dr. Dayton holds multiple degrees, including a Bachelor of Arts in Government, a Master of Public Administration, and Doctorates in Public Administration and Public Health.

His professional journey has spanned various roles, from private business, political & elected office and nonprofit work. Currently, he serves in the Executive Branch of the United States Government working towards a sustainable world.

An accomplished author, Dr. Dayton has published numerous articles and books, addressing key social issues from a scholarly perspective. His work has earned him multiple accolades, including being a recipient of honorary titles such as Nebraska Admiral and a Kentucky Colonel.

Throughout his career, Dr. Dayton has advocated passionately for veterans, advancing their outcomes through legislative advocacy and community partnerships. He believes that security, healthcare, and shelter are keystones to individual dignity, striving to ensure that all veterans have the tools and voice required for post-service success.

Driven by a deep commitment to human rights, Dr. Dayton continues to advocate for healthcare, security, and dignity, drawing on his own experiences as a cancer patient and survivor. His work extends globally, advising several nations and royal houses in capacities that leverage his expertise in policy and advocacy.

Acknowledgments

This book represents not just my thoughts, but a tapestry woven from the threads of many invaluable contributions. I am profoundly thankful to everyone who has been a part of this journey.

Above all, I extend my deepest appreciation to my wife, Erin. Your unwavering support and keen insights have been the backbone of this endeavor. Your patience and love were the light during the darker days of this project, and your perspectives have deeply enriched this work.

I am also grateful to my colleagues from academic and professional circles. Your rigorous debates and constructive critiques have been pivotal in refining the arguments and insights presented in this book.

My heartfelt thanks go out to the courageous veterans who opened up about their experiences. Your profound stories have not only shaped the discussions on public policy and healthcare in this book but also underscored the deeply personal impact of these issues.

A special note of gratitude to my editor and the dedicated publishing team. Your expertise has meticulously sculpted this manuscript into a work that is both polished and accessible. Your commitment was crucial in turning a vision into reality.

Lastly, I thank you, the readers. Your engagement and curiosity fuel the ongoing discourse on social justice and public service. This book is for you, crafted with the hope that it will foster greater understanding and inspire advocacy for the challenges we navigate together.

Dr. Dayton

www.ingramcontent.com/pod-product-compliance
Lightning Source LLC
Chambersburg PA
CBHW032052020426
42335CB00011B/304